Renovation

Restoring the heart and finding home
in the Adirondack Mountains.

for mom
love
jeanne

Coaching assistance by David Hazard,
Ascent: itsyourlifebethere.com
Copyright © 2014 Authored By Jeanne Elizabeth Whyte

ISBN: 1494393115
ISBN 13: 9781494393113

for Mayan, Kinan, and Merri

PROLOGUE

transit: the act of passing over or through; passage
from one place to another. a surveying instrument
for measuring horizontal and vertical angles, con-
sisting of a small telescope mounted on a tripod.

In architectural work, one of the first steps in
designing or restoring a structure is to study the
site plan, or plot survey. This document indi-
cates the position of existing buildings, property
boundaries, and topological features, as if they
were located on a flat surface. To determine this
information, along with various grades or levels of
the property, a transit is used. Built into the transit
is a spirit level, which lets the user know that the
instrument is level and ready.

*S*taring out the window on a cold, stark,
midwinter's afternoon from my kitchen
table, I contemplated the state of my life. Bare

tree branches rustled in the wind and brought on a shiver that chilled me. I knew this season of winter would eventually turn into vibrant spring, and this bleak day would become a starry night, all in good time and in accordance with natural balance. As I thought about the idea of how balance had a way of centering all things in their rightful places, I felt a sense of precarious unbalance in my own life.

The kids were in a good place at university, and my house was calm and peaceful after years of child rearing activities. At the same time though, the bottom seemed to have dropped out of the housing market all over the country, leaving my architectural practice bereft of the steady income I had depended on for over 25 years. The phone just wasn't ringing anymore. I had completely run out of projects to do, and no money had come in for months.

The tremendous and constant demand for an infinite variety of architectural services in Northern Virginia, near Washington, DC, where I lived, had seemingly dissolved. This change had not come about suddenly, but had transpired gradually as an inventory of unsold, abandoned and foreclosed properties continued to accumulate, in what later came to be known as the housing crisis.

For years I had juggled the responsibility of singlehandedly managing my independent practice, while raising two kids alone, and that period of immense effort had suddenly come to an end. My days were now empty, and agonizingly boring.

The bright spark I knew I had been born with was still flickering deep within me. I could feel it smoldering, like an abandoned campfire in the woods sometimes continues to burn underground long after it has been squelched out at the floor of the forest. Was that little spark in danger of being extinguished before I could come up with an idea how to bring it back to life?

I wanted to find my sense of balance again, to adjust the enduring spirit in the depths of my soul. I wanted to clear away the ashes that were obscuring the fire within me, and breathe life into it. The creative impulse of drawing, painting, and my design work had always generated a joyful energy from within, which fueled my artistic passion and happiness. But in the absence of work, and the lack of something significant and creative to do, my mind would repeatedly sink back into the depths of the dilemma I found myself in. I wanted to break through the ground that was holding and smothering me.

I needed to set up a different kind of transit, find a way to bring balance back to my life, and attune to the spirit level.

Had I foreseen the journey on which I was about to embark, I may have allowed fear and uncertainty to bind me steadfastly right to the spot I was in… and I would have missed the most profoundly beautiful, miraculous, and wondrously challenging experience I could ever have imagined.

When you take the path of the soul, you eventually decrease the distance between your ego and your inner divinity, or cosmic spark. As this distance decreases, you become aware of the cosmic spark that exists in every other person and every other entity in the universe. This creates a merging of all things. I refer to this as truth.
— Dharma Singh Khalsa, MD

ONE

*W*hat is the light within, that gives us life and kindles the flame of our passion and will to be? What is the inspiration that pushes us to the next step, even when we don't know where we are going?

We all have it, but at times it feels like that light has gone dormant, like a pilot light that burns softly, invisibly, needing no attention until it goes out.

Only then do we realize how much we need it, and wonder where it went.

Whether nurtured with unconditional love in an environment that grounds us confidently in our magical world, or having suffered an upbringing that has destroyed our will and left us isolated in fear, we have all been subject to human conditioning. Sometimes, as we mature, a breakthrough occurs where it suddenly becomes clear — maybe in a flash of insight — that conditioning has dominated our perspective for too long, and we long to return to the cosmic spark that brought us precious life in the first place.

My spark was always about love, beauty, and art. I knew that I saw things in a unique way even from the time I was a little child. I wanted to be good, because there was something very good inside me, that I identified with. I somehow recognized that there was a core of love within everything, and it was beautiful. Maybe that was why I wanted to make that beauty shine through for others to see. At first it was by coloring and drawing, then by watercolor painting and photography. If the picture was no good, I threw it away.

Eventually I was led through my artwork into architecture, first by drawing and painting houses, and later by learning how to design them for people to live in. I loved making wonderfully open, light filled places. As my experience designing houses evolved, I saw that bringing sunlight and nature right into a house created a sense of well-being that would add to the happiness of those who would live there.

Living in a quaint little Quaker village called Lincoln, in Loudoun County, Virginia, I'd had an ongoing architectural practice for many years. I had seen the area grow from an endless expanse of pristine horse country, dotted with small villages and historic old towns, to a sprawling smear of way too big houses everywhere, obliterating what had been endless rolling farmland. My passion for a making beautiful houses had begun to flicker because the sprawl went on and so did the explosion of big boxy houses. Sensitive planning was practically non-existent, except for the very few high density planned neighborhoods, which preserved green space, in the northern part of the county. The opportunity to do the kind of work I wanted to do had slipped away.

Carefully planned, modestly sized houses with natural materials, made for growing, evolving families and environmental conservation, were of no interest to builders and realtors who depended on the newly rich customer and his need to show off success with a mansion. People were calling them McMansions, because on either side of any road they stretched far and wide, all the same — huge houses for a handful of people to live in them, on large lots that had only recently been pastureland, and no natural landscape to soften or conceal their boring sameness.

Having done many years of my apprenticeship on Hilton Head Island in the 70's, environmentally sensitive, carefully site integrated design was something that came naturally to me. While working for small independent firms on the island, I learned that site considerations were paramount to good residential design. When we designed a home there, trees were left in place close enough to touch the walls and roofs. All elements of the site, such as natural grade, vegetation, rivers, streams, creeks, wetlands, existing historical features, and the proximity to the ocean itself, were carefully evaluated so that they could be protected and preserved, and could actually enhance the connection of the new home with its natural environment. Design review committees studied each project to see that by conforming to established guidelines, every home would blend into the landscape and compliment the inherent beauty of the island. This respect for the environment and our connection to it exemplified Hilton Head Island as a model of responsible design and site planning. What I learned there was such an integral part of my early training that it was second nature to me.

The homes I learned to create on Hilton Head Island rose gently behind the protected dunes, and nestled into the palm and palmetto landscape with soft, natural colors and materials native to the coastal lowlands. They were respectful of the ongoing erosion of the ocean's shoreline, and were kept to a minimal footprint, the main level set significantly above sea level to discourage flooding by ocean storm surges. That kind of design sensitivity was something I carried with me everywhere thereafter.

The abomination of what had been done in Loudoun County was troubling, and getting worse. Over the years I had attempted to work for private clients rather than for builders, because at least with individuals there was some hope to be able to influence them to consider the natural conditions of a site and encourage them to build an appropriate, environmentally conscious home that would enhance the relationship between the family and the natural world, not cut them off from it. The custom home market was very limited though, because most of the large parcels of farmland had been scooped up by investors and developers who wanted to get in there with a sure thing, a subdivision, and get out with their money.

The home buyer, usually a couple where both would be commuting to DC or the beltway areas to work, really had little choice but to select from the uninspired offerings, fake "colonials" with a little brick on the front side only, vinyl siding everywhere else, and of course the usual curved staircase in a two story foyer, meant to impress visitors. Very few couples had the time or patience to build a custom home, nor the understanding of why they should do so. They had no real concept of the positive impact a conscientiously designed home would have on their life.

Historic houses are a unique design challenge because there is usually something beautifully old and authentic to restore, even if is necessary to renovate some areas of the house to meet the needs of today's modern families. Renovations, restorations and additions had been my bread and butter projects and had provided me with steady work for years. I was proud of that work. To be able to restore and preserve the elegance of a very old home, built by the early Americans, and delicately add space to it so that it functioned smoothly for a modern, active lifestyle was a skill I had carefully honed.

When the "housing bubble" began to grow, people just wanted to quickly get in on it and buy something. They had every expectation that their investment would be solid and guaranteed. After all, they saw houses selling on the very first day of their listing, with multiple purchase offers, some for more than the asking price. How could you lose?

We all know how, now. Banks and lenders were doling out loans like candy to kids, and many of them went to not really qualified buyers, with nothing to fall back on if one of them lost their job. Monthly payments were sky high but nobody expected to lose their job, come on hard times, or heaven forbid, have their house lose value and place them in a situation where they owed more on it than it was worth. Then lose their job.

Naturally, when the inventory of repossessed, unsold and often empty houses began to rise, there was very little work for architects. Many of my friends who were in practice were finding they had to lay off employees, and even close their offices. Like me, they had almost nothing to do, but unlike them, I had no employees to lay off, and no office to close. I had built a lovely modest place to work that was attached to my house through a mudroom. I just wanted to be in there working.

Now that work was just gone. It didn't look like it would ever really come back either, because most of the land was gone too. What were my options?

It felt like my career had gone from the brightness of success, to the cold ashes of an abandoned fire. If I didn't find a way to rekindle it, I would find myself in serious jeopardy. After all, the bills just kept coming in, and all of my financial obligations demanded my attention.

I had tried to think of a creative solution, but nothing seemed workable. The ground was beginning to crumble beneath me. The only thing I could think of was to get some sort of job in another field like a clerk, grocery checker or house cleaner, but even those positions were impossible to get with so many people unemployed, searching for work.

I spent a lot of time at the kitchen table in my old rocker, because the sun came streaming in there, making my dilemma bearable while I pondered, wondering what to do. It was hard to believe that my practice of twenty-five years was disintegrating before me. Somehow I had to find a way to change the course of my life instead of allowing these external events to drive me further into despair, loneliness and financial ruin. The foundation was cracking, for sure, but did I need to build something entirely new? It sure looked as if the old structure was seriously damaged to the point that maybe it was beyond repair, but what could I do about it? I had a great little home to care for, that I had designed especially for myself and two energetic teenagers. But there were quite a few more years to go before the financial burden of their education would be over, and I had a failing business to deal with.

One day when I was feeling especially thoughtful about what to do with my off-centered life, I got an unexpected call from a friend. Tina, who lived in the Adirondacks, suggested that if I had nothing to do, why not just get in the car and come up to New York?

When the universe has a new idea for your future, it can be with a stunning sense of humor. Tina had an appointment for a colonoscopy a few days hence, and thought it would be the perfect excuse for me to come see her and be with her for the test. I thought the idea was a little crazy — going so far to accompany her for a relatively simple medical procedure - but maybe I should go to the aid of my friend, and just get away for a bit to see if any fresh ideas came to mind.

I owned a little dilapidated lakefront camp near her house, and had future plans to renovate it and make a new home there some day, but I had intended to get my kids through school first so I could feel free to leave Virginia and move to New York for the empty nest phase of my life. It was such an exciting an idea for me that I had already done a set of plans, and they were ready to go for whenever the right time came.

It had never occurred to me that the time might be now — I wasn't ready!

A little light sparked on in my head. Be in the moment. Step into the river of life. Go with the flow — all concepts I had been learning for years.

Was this really my answer? Go now? Go on up there and renovate the camp right now, and make myself a job out of it? On the other hand, I couldn't just keep sitting here in my rocker waiting for the economy to improve and the phone to ring.

I called Tina back and asked her if she knew of any place near my own camp where I could stay for awhile, that had heat. After all it was February, and my camp, like most of those in the Adirondacks, was not winterized, and had no heat. In fact, it had no foundation at all. I told her about my idea, while inwardly wondering whether I had lost my senses, but she was excited too!

I knew the scheme was a little crazy, but she liked it, and wanted to check with some friends who had a camp right near mine. She called back within the hour.

"Some close friends of mine," she said, "within walking distance of your camp, are willing to let you stay in their place, in exchange for covering the utility bills while you're there!"

It was so amazing that they would make this offer. I was stunned. They didn't even know me, but based on Tina's referral they said I could come and stay at their place right away if I wanted to.

When I hung up the phone I felt a great thud in my chest. A door had opened for me just when I needed it. I could literally just drop everything I was doing, in fact my whole life, and go.

What was I thinking? This was crazy! My parents, family and friends were sure to think I had lost my mind. My kids would probably be for it, but they were pretty open minded when it came to imaginative ideas.

I had met a few contractors up there but basically did not know any of the people I would need to rely on for the subcontracting of all the trades to re-build my camp. I would have to create new contacts and form new relationships. Over the years I had managed the construction of many houses, renovations and additions for my own clients with designs I had done for them. But starting out to do this in a totally new locale would not be easy for a newcomer. A new face means more competition for established contractors, and most of them do not want to work with people they don't know, especially a woman. It would be an extremely challenging undertaking, to say the least, and I didn't see emotional support coming from anywhere. Could I really just pick up a bag, grab the dog and take off 500 miles into the northern wilderness alone?

I sensed that the decision to get up and leave my home, my established architectural practice in Virginia, and the life I knew, was to become the true turning point of everything... it was as if my future was balanced on the fulcrum of this very moment.

Before my mind could catch up with everything I was imagining and dreaming... I ran upstairs to pack a small bag so I could leave early in the morning.

And just like that, I made a decision that would lead to the greatest project I'd ever undertaken, the renovation of my entire life.

*We seem to think that beginning is setting out from
a lonely point along some line of direction
into the unknown. This is not the case.
Shelter and energy come alive when a beginning is embraced.
Goethe says that once the commitment is made,
destiny conspires with us to support and realize it.*
— John O'Donahue

Two

Leaning toward the windshield as if trying to see the future, all I could see was pure white. Swirling snow blew furiously and covered everything including the road itself so that there was no distinction between it and the landscape beyond. Evening was closing in on my nine-hour trek north in the dead of winter, and it was so icy cold out that the heater had been running steadily the whole way.

Would I be able to make it to the cabin before snow closed the roads ahead of me? There would be no more motels to stop in at, and the idea of spending the night alone in the storm on the side of the road was frightening. As the heavy snow continued, and evening began to descend, I wondered if I would get there that night. I tried to stretch my shoulders back a little to ease the rigid position I was in, while my hands clenched the steering wheel. I was scared.

There were only a few more hours to the Adirondack camp where I was hoping heat was on in anticipation of my arrival, but what about the steep driveway? Even if I made it there, would I have to go down the hill on foot from the road to the door? It would surely be dark by then, and I hadn't thought to bring a flashlight. This is what happens when you suddenly fly off like a madwoman to take up residence alone in the wilderness.

The tension in my back from struggling to see where I was going had turned into unrelenting pain, but the snowfall finally began to soften and I could actually take a couple of deep breaths of relief. I pushed forward along the lonely road without another car in sight, through the homesteads and dairy farms of central New York that stretched ahead beneath the darkening sky.

When the car crept down the long declining road into the Mohawk Valley, I realized it would be less than an hour before I would enter the southwest corner of the 6 million acre Adirondack Park. Crossing that point was always a joy on every trip I had ever made to camp. It meant the hectic real world would be left behind me, and my place of endless lakes and mountains, bald eagles, bears and otters — peace and solitude — was before me.

When at last I entered the park, the lights of houses became sparse and the road began to wind between frozen white lakes and dark winter woods, taking me up into the mountains.

Darkness had fallen when I finally reached the top of the driveway which marked the entrance to my new temporary home. It was certainly isolated, but I was so grateful to Tina's friends for their generosity in offering to let me stay there. My own rustic cabin would be like a little ice chest right now.

As I brought the car to a halt, I peered apprehensively down through the night woods at the secluded camp below. A smile spread all over my face when I saw golden porch lights glowing, and that the steep driveway had been recently plowed. I said a silent prayer of thanks to the mysterious person who had made sure the driveway was cleared of the daylong snowfall. Even in the pitch darkness I could see that there was probably two feet of snow on the ground beneath the trees in the deep woods that surrounded me. Everything in the landscape was covered in a white cloak and the snow had begun to fall again.

Even with the porch lights beckoning, I felt a twinge of fear as I imagined how I would have to steer my vehicle down the steep hill, and around a hairpin turn to make it to the back door. A sudden image flashed in my mind — of sliding sideways into the woods, out of control, and onto the frozen lake below. Holding my breath, I went for it. In low gear four wheel drive I crept right down to the stoop, and brought the car to a gentle halt. A long sigh of relief escaped me, and my little dog, Iona, started leaping around in an attempt to signal that she was more than ready to jump out.

I was more than ready too. The tension of the previous hours had taken its toll and I was as stiff as a 90 year old. Tentatively, I opened the car door and awkwardly came to my feet.

The back door was unlocked. Lights were on inside too. I had never seen the place so every step within was a revelation, and I was stunned at the warmth and coziness of it.

A quick tour revealed a beautiful log vaulted great room, with a fire thoughtfully laid and ready to be lit in the big stone fireplace. There was a generous kitchen with center island, tons of work-space and a wood cookstove. A small master suite right there on the main level would make it possible to consolidate everything on the first floor. The entire place was made of pine, every plank cut from the vast forest around me. I inhaled the sweet fragrance of wood, and began to finally relax with each breath.

It was easy to unload the meager belongings I had brought with me, get inside, and secure the door against the freezing darkness. Iona ran all around to explore every nook and cranny. It was surprisingly warm inside the camp — the heat had been turned up for my arrival! I lit the fire, some candles and little lamps, and began to unpack the things I needed for the night. My own blankets, linens and towels made me feel comfortable in the new surroundings. After the bed was made up with familiar sheets and quilts, it looked as welcoming as... home.

The relief of finally arriving after hours of struggle hit me, and I was suddenly exhausted, but so glad to be there. As tense as it had been, this journey into the night was the beginning of something new — I felt it in my bones.

Turning out the last light that night brought home the sense that I was really alone in the dark snowy wilderness. Where I had come from, there was always a streetlight on in the lane, activity in the neighbor's houses, and the constant din of cars on the roads so nearby. Not here. This was truly being a woman alone and in silence. No tv to provide company. I concentrated on the warmth and safety of the little bedroom and drove out the imaginings of dangerous animals stalking out there in the dark woods.

And yet as the fire continued to crackle and pop softy as it died down, I settled beneath the piles of blankets and felt the peace of the place. I said a prayer of thankfulness to have made it, and wondered what would happen next. A blessed sleep overtook me.

When the sun peeked down through the canopy of trees outside the next morning, I slipped on my old robe and went out to the kitchen to put on the kettle and look around at my surroundings in the dawn light. I knew immediately how lucky I was to be there. Sunlight began to spill in through the windows, turning the worn wood floors into a rich, gleaming gold. The pine walls glowed.

Moments later, mug of tea in cupped hands, I went back to my room and plumped up the pillows so I could rest against them and sip the warming liquid for a few moments of contemplation, a precious time I always took for myself each morning. Through the window beside me I could see the woods in the emerging daylight. Everything was covered with new fallen snow. The lake, just a stone's throw from the house, was frozen solid. A sheet of white spread all the way to the distant shoreline, with its blown pines and the soft, blue-gray mountains behind them. Bright snow came up the steps from the forest floor and onto a wide deck that wrapped the house with a flawless, sparkling skirt of white.

This place allowed the space for silence. Somewhere in the camp wood creaked with the dryness of warmth, as loud as a stranger's footstep. Or so it seemed. The intensity of the quietness made every little sound seem like an intrusion. I had spent time in the Adirondacks in winter, but this was the first time I had come with the understanding that I would be by myself, looking out and experiencing its vast wildness.

As I sipped warm tea, began to unpack and moved things around a little to suit my stay, I couldn't help but wonder what I was doing there. With no visible means of support, many hours and miles away from my children and not much understanding from my family, I was really following the inclinations of my heart. Where was this adventure going to take me? It was a path I was unused to following. I had absolutely no plan, and really no idea where my heart was leading me, but it felt good anyway.

I remembered a time when I was very small, before I had any siblings, I made a tiny house for myself between the two metal screen curtains that hung on each side of a see-through fireplace between the kitchen and living room of my parents' first house. I felt so comfortable there in my own little space, hidden, but yet in the perfect place to be able to look out at the big world.

Something inside me called for my own special place, where I could be safe just being me, and I had been trying to create that sacred place of belonging all of my life.

That first morning alone in the deep woods, I had the twinkling of a feeling that I was on the verge of finding that place at last.

I had lived nearby as a child, just an hour away at Lake Delta, near Rome, New York, in a small stone cottage right beside the lake. My childhood days were spent right on the lake, swimming, canoeing and waterskiing all summer, and riding bikes with the other kids wherever we wanted to go. In winter, sledding, tobogganing and skating kept us so warm inside that we never noticed the cold that lasted so many months.

From the outside, our family seemed perfect. Under the surface though, was an underlying current of aloneness, emotional suppression, and even neglect. My parents were distant, and preferred that we keep out of their way. So, we kids tried to do exactly what was expected of us. There were no screaming arguments or temper tantrums, but neither was there the loving tenderness and attention that all children need and long for. We simply went about our young lives being good as we were told to be, while our feelings remained hidden. No one cared how we felt, and we knew those feelings didn't matter.

Throughout my childhood my dad would make pancakes for breakfast on Saturday mornings. I remember one Saturday he was playing an album of my mom's favorite singer, Andy Williams, on the hi-fi. When the song "Danny Boy" started to play, I was overwhelmed with emotion at hearing the words of love and devotion, and ran crying to my room to hide my tears. My dad came to the bedroom door and demanded to know what was wrong with me and why was I crying? I couldn't answer anything but "I don't know", because I didn't understand the deep emotional connection that song was making with my young broken heart. I just wanted to be held and loved for who I was, a thing I felt impossible to ask for, or have.

I don't remember ever having a hug, a kiss, or an "I love you", not even when going to bed at night. The most I could hope for was a perfunctory peck that pretty much missed my cheek when I went to say goodnight to Mom or Dad. Then it would be the dawn of another day of trying to deserve to be loved, but there was never the reward I always hoped for. Every time love was denied, it felt like cold ashes of hope were falling onto the inborn spark of my spirit, smothering it. If only that spark had been nourished and brought to life — if only that fire had been tended.

The underlying spirit in my heart was struggling to say I was already good enough just as I was, but the physical reality was that I somehow didn't measure up. These conflicting impulses made me silence that inner voice, for survival, and that kind of conditioning led to a lifetime of confusion.

Children were given a lot of freedom to roam all over the natural world at that time, because the fear of a child being taken and all the dangers kids might face in today's scary world hadn't kicked in yet. We swam in the lake for hours unsupervised. We took boats out, overturned them and played beneath them, listening to the echoes of our own voices and staring into the amazing underwater haven below us. The natural world was our playground, and we immersed ourselves in its soothing, healing powers.

There was nothing like a cool, soft swim underwater to make everything feel okay. In the silence of the deep green world, I could hear my own heart beating loudly. I felt the sense of separateness and alienation from my parents, but I could also choose the solace nature could bring me. I could actually feel the inner radiance that was pounding to free itself, and knew there was something special within me that was dying to live.

When I was about 12 years old, my dad took a new job at the Pentagon in Washington that tore us away from our beautiful place on the lake. We moved to a Virginia subdivision, and our entire lives changed. We kids felt so abandoned in the new place. Dad was always gone with his new job, and Mom seemed to have no idea what we kids needed. We had to remake our lives as best we could, find new friends and a way to suffer the oppressive heat and humidity of the barren new place. Our playground by the lake was gone.

I was a "good girl" as long as I did what was expected of me, and that was to conform to the pattern my parents set before me as acceptable for the family. And for girls. But that pattern did not coincide with my true nature and the longings in my heart.

From the time I could lift a pencil I was fascinated by drawing, coloring, and painting — making something new and beautiful. I loved to see what unique things would emerge when interesting elements were brought together. I was forever drawing something, even in the schoolroom. My teachers seemed to tolerate this and would even ask to see what I had drawn when class was over. Then they started making me do their bulletin boards for them — I had a playful sense of imagination that came naturally to me, and it was useful when they just couldn't manage to come up with anything interesting to make the classrooms and halls more lively. Meanwhile, I took oil and watercolor painting lessons, helped with the high school periodical illustrations, and became president of the Art Guild, an after school club. I even began to participate in shows and sell some of my work.

Artwork was okay for girls...or for doodling around in your spare time, but when it came time to choosing a career and going to college, it was not okay to declare, "I want to study art." To my dad, the acceptable vocations for me were to be a teacher, nurse, or secretary.

Despite my father's refusal to allow me to go to art school, on my own I had applied to three terrific universities with great art programs, and was thrilled to have been accepted by all of them. No go. My parents decided that I had to go to an in-state school and study the humanities they thought were best for me. At that time these were all girls schools, so I chose Mary Washington College, the then female part of University of Virginia. There was approval and even a little excitement about this......for my parents. On the day they dropped me off there, the distinct feeling of forlorn disappointment settled over me like a weight on my chest, an emptiness in my heart. Sitting alone on the single bed in my new dorm room, I felt isolated and desolate when they left. I knew no one and had no enthusiasm for the program of study I was supposed to be enthusiastic about. It was impossible to even select classes that interested me because there was nothing offered that I really wanted to pursue! My own passions had been pushed aside for what I had to do to obtain my parents' approval. There weren't even any electives in drawing or painting – just one art history class. I selected that. It all made me feel sad.

As I reflected on these old memories I realized that to construct a house for my own precious soul to inhabit, to live in with joy and passion, attending that college and building my life around my parents' vision for me was the beginning of building the wrong house for me.

Even knowing I was making a big mistake didn't give me the courage to correct the course I was on, however. In my entire life the need for love, acceptance and approval led me to believe I always had to be good enough in my parents' eyes to earn it. Like many overachievers of my age, being smart, making honor society, and always trying to do my very best without too much notice from anyone, never seemed to have any effect on my parents. They expected it. The loving affection and acceptance I longed for never came.

Ignoring my own voice was something I did so habitually that I didn't even know I was doing it. I was afraid to cry when I was upset, too self-conscious to laugh aloud when I was happy, and I carefully hid my feelings of sadness at not being free to be who I was. I wanted to be me, but somehow the me that I was, was not who my parents wanted me to be. So, I tried to be who they wanted me to be, so they would love me. What overpowered my inner voice was the false security of approval, which took the place of the authentic love and unconditional acceptance I longed for.

My parents would probably have been shocked to have known this conflict existed in me, I'm sure, because I was afraid to speak about it. Every morning I woke up with a determination to be the best person I could, going about my days just like everyone else was. It was only underneath my conditioned personality that I felt the murmurings of my own real heart and spirit.

In that first college semester, away from my parents for the first time, I began to hear that voice struggling to be heard, and I was listening. In the silence of my dorm room, while everyone was studying late at night, I made a flower and vine covered drawing with all the words of George Harrison's song —

> "Try to realize it's all within yourself.
> no one else can make you change...
>
> And to see you're really only very
> small
> and life goes on within you and
> without you..."

Every word of the Beatle's song Within You and Without You seemed to have been written just for me. I hung the drawing over my bed to remind me every day of my intuition that all the love I needed was within me. If only I could have held on to the truth in those words...

I shook myself from my reverie as the brightness of morning emerged, suffusing the pretty room with light. The woods all around and the lake below beckoned me to explore my new mountain home. I got dressed and pulled on some socks and boots, mittens and a warm coat, and headed out for a walk with Iona running ahead of me.

Outside in the crisp, icy air, Iona scampered down the hill as though she had done it a million times, while I proceeded more cautiously behind her through powdery snow and frosted pines. Sun sparkled between the dark trunks I used to keep my balance navigating the steep hill, and at last we reached the shore and looked across the ice. The freezing air filled my body with refreshment and renewal.

The lake was a sheet of white all the way to the isolated island beyond, and the far shore in the distance. Little birds fluttered in the trees, leaving a mist of snow in their wake. As Iona ran fearlessly everywhere exploring and sniffing all the brand new things she had never encountered before, I took in the magnificence of the setting. It was a wonderland.

Our lives awaken through ordinary magic
— Chogyam Trungpa Rinpoche

Three

Outside, I was caught up in thought as I stepped through the deep bright snow in the woods. I wanted to be fully in the moment, but somehow the past seemed to be speaking to me, urgently. What insight was struggling to make itself known?

Like many girls in college, I had been desperate for love. The main topic was who was pairing up with whom and what we girls could do to get our very own boyfriend. Since I didn't feel at all lovable, I thought my case was hopeless. The only thing I thought I had to offer was the immense amount of love I had to give. It couldn't be about me, so it had to be what I could give some one else.

This overwhelming sense of unworthiness led me to a series of wrong choices and bad relationships, one after another. Eventually, I decided I was incapable of making those kinds of choices anymore. Every time I had chosen for myself, it had been wrong, and I when I looked back on my own history I realized that I had never received the touch of real love in a relationship, or in a marriage. My conditioned sense of inadequacy was the basis from which I always chose a partner who I loved, but who didn't love me, much less in a way that fostered my spiritual growth and wellbeing. In other words, I had always tried to earn love by my actions.

I didn't want to do that ever again. The impact of that insight was startling! Even as an architect who created gorgeous homes for all my clients, I had built my own life on the wrong foundations — trying to be good enough to be loved. Could I leave this lifelong ingrained habit behind, along with the rest of my old life? Could I

34

begin to create a life and a new home that would reflect who I really was?

Back at the cabin door, Iona and I both shook off the snow as best we could and went into the cozy warmth, with a bundle of kindling sticks for the fireplace. I set my boots and mittens out to dry, hung my coat on a hook, and filled the kettle for hot tea. There was nothing I really had to accomplish on that first day, so I brought the kindling into the great room, laid a new fire, grabbed a warm throw and settled onto a comfortable sofa.

Gazing into the crackling fire, I thought about the many times I had worked so hard for love, and how much of myself I had given away. With a sense of deep aching sadness, I pondered the depths of my heart to search out the truth about who I had become in all the useless effort I had made over a lifetime. In my sense of unworthiness, I literally became the person I thought my loved one needed — after all, who would love me the way I was?

My very first boyfriend, whom I met while still just a freshman in college, made me feel loved. When he put his arms around me it felt like a home I had longed for all of my life. At last

I felt I had found the affection and acceptance I so needed. We were inseparable, and when we discovered a baby was coming we delighted in the prospect of setting up a tiny apartment for three in Charlottesville, where he was completing a pre-med degree. We got married.

It didn't last. I found myself leaving after four short years to set off on my own, with my little girl, headed to Hilton Head. I was fearless then, because I had no idea how hard it would be. I just wanted to be safe and happy and I was full of optimism.

For years while I worked and raised my child, I explored relationships that never seemed to work out. I was always choosing the wrong man, because I didn't really know what real love was. Constantly, I was willing to mold myself into what some one else needed, so they would love me, putting my own needs aside for theirs.

When I finally returned to Virginia years later, I met a man who let me know almost right from the beginning that he had an ongoing relationship with something that barely allowed room for anyone or anything else in his life.

Even so, it did not discourage me. One night when he had invited me to his apartment, he returned from a trip to the bathroom visibly altered. He was informing me quite dramatically of what his life was made of. A feeling of disappointment, disgust and nausea rose from the pit of my stomach. I decided to go home – the evening was over for me.

He was exposing his true self, to see if I was going to be ready willing and able to tolerate something negative, something that would hurt me deeply, that he had no intention of changing. The relationship was going to come with all his habits intact, or there would be no relationship.

I may have ignored him for a few days, while in my mind I began to justify his behavior and how I could handle it. I told myself that love could overcome anything. It could heal the emotional pain he was obviously suffering from. He didn't deserve to be abandoned to battle it alone; he needed the vast, all encompassing love I could give him, to make him realize how beautiful life could really be. Love could solve anything, and I knew I had that kind of love, even if he didn't. By loving him more than anyone else ever had, I believed I could earn his love in return. As usual, I put my real feelings aside.

My design work and his carpentry skill seemed to blend so perfectly together. Before long we were inspired to make use of this creative combination, and began a hand-built passive solar cabin together in the woods. When it was finished, we moved in and got married there.

Our marriage was doomed from day one because of my illusionary thinking. I already had my architectural practice going, but expanded this to include building construction, so we could work together. My work schedule was in place, designing, drawing, meeting with clients and managing projects, but I found as time went by that he had no work schedule. Work for him was intermittent, not a priority, and over time it continued to diminish. I went to work at my in-town office bright and early every day, never knowing exactly how he spent his time. I figured he was going to the projects we were working on, at a reasonable time, and spending most of every day doing carpentry.

In my mind there was a justification for everything he did. Whenever I had doubts or hesitations, I determined to love him more, so that everything would work out. I had a huge capacity for overlooking reality, a habit well practiced for my entire life.

One day a worker came to me and told me that my husband was showing up at a project site once a day and then was gone for the rest of the day, while I assumed he was on site all day working with and the directing the crew. No one knew how he was spending his days, not even me. We had a 4-wheel drive work truck that was purchased new and paid off, and that disappeared, having been traded in without my knowledge or permission for a bigger brand new truck that he wanted, which was soon repossessed for lack of his payments.

In time we had two precious little children, but their care fell completely to me even though I was working all the time. I struggled to maintain the business we had together, but was constantly losing ground. When I asked what was going on with him, there was silence. We were no longer communicating on any level, and life was utterly miserable. I put up with the situation, constantly looking for ways in which I could change, so that everything would somehow be okay.

The downhill cycle I'd committed myself to continued until our existence together and everything we held dear became jeopardized. Our relationship, home and property, the business… everything was about to go down the drain.

I began to agonize over how I had gotten the opposite of what I had wanted. I begged him to make changes but he was unwilling. Even counseling could not help us because the relationship was completely one sided. I wanted to work and try at it but he wanted nothing but to be left alone so that he could go on doing whatever he wanted. He let me know that I had no right to expect or even think otherwise, because he had never promised me anything, not even his faithfulness.

He was right. All the promises, hopes and dreams had come from me. He was just along for the ride. The counselor finally told me truthfully that I was grasping a sinking ship. This man didn't love me and had no intention of meeting any of my needs or requirements. I had done all the work in the relationship, and where had it gotten me? I realized I was going to have to leave.

Even though my heart was directing me, my rational mind was displaying conflicting signals. Why give up on the marriage? Why not just keep on trying to do everything, so I wouldn't have to face starting over alone with two little kids? I didn't want to admit even to myself what a big mistake I had made, again. I wanted to glaze over the reality of what was, and immerse myself in the daily care of the kids, and work, so I wouldn't have to do what I had to do – confront the immense problem of facing the fact that my husband didn't love me, never did, and the storm of realities that came with that realization.

To survive this, I would have to be a different person than I ever had been, even though I had been through divorce before. This time there was everything to lose, that hadn't already been lost. My marriage, the business we had together, my work, and a beautiful home I had designed and we had built would be gone. How could I have allowed myself to get into a relationship where I was valued so minimally?

Here was the most painful part.

I somehow knew that I had been complicit in going against my self. To have the love I wanted I had again accepted a situation that had no connection with the spirit within me. I had denied that voice — the energy of my heart. My own light was buried so deeply that I couldn't even see it anymore.

Now how would I manage to raise two little children, just 12 months and 3, who were looking up to me for all the care and love they so needed, just as I had? I didn't want them to follow a path of degradation and the absence of a nurturing love. There had to be a way to resurrect my own heart and soul, and bring the light of that love to life for myself and for them. I would have to go deep inside myself to find a new way. I would have to rebuild everything alone, from the bottom up, like digging the footings for a new life and then starting the new foundation.

What followed were years of fearful trauma, turmoil, and the intense amount of determined effort it takes to break away from everything known, to raise two very small kids, while working to support us somehow. There was no help from anywhere. The business was closed and I had to start over again with my independent architectural practice. My husband refused to help me at all. My family looked the other way as if nothing was happening. The economy was in recession and available work was minimal.

Each day was like taking another baby step, fraught with doubts and anxiety. Thankfully, my older daughter was already attending college with the support of her paternal grandmother. She was happy to be in another state far away from the chaos my life had become.

I had to move from place to place — rooms we shared in someone's house, to tiny rented house one after another, six times before my then five year old son entered the first grade (and my daughter was still only 3). Everywhere we went to live was so small, so cold and so difficult. There were many tears, and the grief over so much loss was tremendous. I had to pull myself together every day to somehow meet with clients, draw lovely houses for other people, and make a living.

While life went on I had to present a cheerful face for my little ones and hold back the sorrow till they went to sleep at night when I could finally release the agony that plagued me constantly. I had to find a way out of my own grief.

I read all the spiritual writings I could find, late into the nights, looking for the answers. There had to be an answer somewhere, but I had no idea where. This was my problem, and if I was to survive, I had to solve it alone. There was no help from anyone.

Through Marianne Williamson I discovered the Course in Miracles, and began to find new ways of seeing God. I began to see that God was within me, and that by identifying and embracing this loving spirit, I could soothe my broken heart and begin to heal. Once this concept became real for me, I was desperate to know more about it. I read all the Buddhist teachers of the day, Chogyam Trungpa, Pema Chodran, Jack Kornfield, John Welwood, Thich Knat Hahn, Ram Dass, and many others, and began to explore the practice of meditation. I had learned transcendental meditation years previously, but I found new meaning in using meditation as a means of attaining some sort of control over my run away emotions, to regain balance. I began to bring the concept of mindful awareness into my life.

Without realizing it, I was creating a new spiritual foundation, and this time it would be set on a solid base. The strength of it was my understanding that the truth of God is within us — the light of love, compassion and mindfulness is always within to guide us. It is not something we have to earn, it is already there, because we are born with it. My heart was calling out and I was finally there to hear it, and answer. I was no longer denying my own truth and hiding from the painful lack of love and acceptance I had always felt, I was living it. There was no place left to go, nothing to do but just be there with the pain that was so real, begin to move through it, and find a way to let it go.

Just before and during these years of struggle, something positive had also happened. Years before, an architect on Hilton Head Island, who had hired me to do all of his renderings, had taken an interest in me. He taught me how to diagram a house design according to its site, orientation, and program — to fit this design sensitively into the environment, and execute construction documents. After working with him for about five years I went on to work in many other architectural offices, continuing my apprenticeships, design awareness and overall experience. There came a point in time when I realized that even without a degree in architecture, I could prepare to take the three day qualification exam, which if passed, would allow me to sit for the three day NCARB exam a year after that, leading to architectural licensure. I decided to aim for this.

Documentation of college credit and the 13 years of apprenticeship with licensed architects I already had under my belt needed to be presented along with lots of other requirements, in order to be accepted as a candidate. I had to get in touch with everyone I had ever worked with and get official verifications and letters of recommendation from all of them.

After getting everything in order, and studying by myself almost every night after working all day for architects, with texts I was able to get from universities, I took the three day qualifying test and passed it. I was so thrilled to be in line for the NCARB the following spring! That was an exam of extreme challenge and endurance for anyone facing it. Sometimes it took years to pass, like the law boards do. It was also a three day exam. The design section is a 12 hour marathon beginning at 6 am and continuing until 6 pm, on the third day, where candidates have to design a complete building, like an airport or student center, and execute drawings for it.

Architecture wasn't one of those professions suitable for girls, I remembered. It took a side of the brain females just don't have developed, emotional and vulnerable as we girls are. Well, I was about to show them all differently. I knew I could do it with the amount of bold-faced determination I could muster up. Basically, I didn't even share my plan with my family, because I knew I would not be encouraged.

One day I opened my mailbox and in it was a letter informing me that I had passed all areas of the NCARB exam, and licenses for both DC and Virginia were forthcoming. It was one of the most exciting, elating moments of my life, made all the better for knowing the obstacles I had overcome to get there, alone. I was ready to begin my own independent practice, doing work I loved, and still do to this day. I don't think anyone could have ever fully understood the depth of the happiness I felt for following my instincts, doing something I wanted and knew I could do, though it seemed impossible, and succeeding in such a big way.

It was almost a private triumph though, because I had worked so hard for many years, behind the scenes, following my passion for art and architecture. Some of the architects I had worked for in the run up for taking my exams just loved the skillful, valuable renderings I had done for them because they themselves could barely even draw, but they didn't really believe I would ever be licensed and have my own firm. When I ventured to share with them my dreams of designing environmentally conscious houses, of natural materials, they scoffed and called me "overconfident". Meanwhile I suffered the harassment of being pressured to have relationships with some of the married partners.

It was a bittersweet feeling to find that I had accomplished a momentous goal in passing those exams, for no one really believed in my determination to transform my natural skill into a dynamic career. As soon as I was licensed I opened my own private practice.

I had done it on my own.

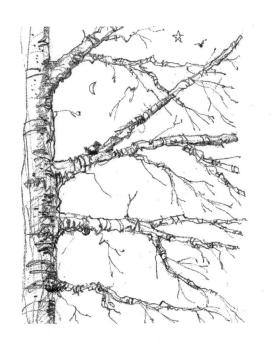

We have to be willing to change.
When we begin to tame the movement of our mind,
it affects everything else.
It's like renovating: once you start it's hard to stop.
— Sakyong Mipham

Four

I met my friend Tina when a mutual friend I had done work for at The Hedges at Blue Mountain Lake, further to the East in the park, referred her to me. When I first came up to meet and consult with her about a new camp she wanted to build, she was living on Seventh Lake. On that very first day, after our initial meeting, she took me on an exploratory boat ride all around Seventh Lake, and I fell in love with it. Our shared adoration of historic old camps and a fascination with being on the water in the wilderness with all its creatures created a bond between us that has endured.

As we worked together through the process of designing her new place, we always planned for an outing together on the water after our work session was done. She loved to kayak and introduced me to one of her boats. I absolutely loved kayaking after having been a canoeist all my life, so we took as many kayaking trips as we could together, just to be out on the lakes. She knew that I was looking for a small waterfront place to buy, and she was always on the lookout for something uniquely affordable for me.

On one trip to meet with her and spend a little time in the Adirondacks, Tina told me she had seen a hand scribbled "for sale" sign on a post across the lake from her place, and urged me to paddle one of her kayaks over and take a look at it. I couldn't resist the idea. I climbed into one of her old Necky kayaks and crossed directly over the main part of the lake. There was a little wind up, and I had to paddle hard to keep going straight over, but I was dying of curiosity. I wondered what sort of place it could be, that I hadn't yet noticed a sign from the road. I discovered later that the owners didn't want any pressure from realtors and were hoping one of their lake neighbors would take an interest, so they had never listed the place.

Seventh Lake is the 7th of a series of eight connected lakes called the Fulton Chain of Lakes, which begins at Old Forge and continues northeast to just past Inlet, in the central Adirondacks. They are all pristine, crystal clear, wilderness lakes that meander between mountains that surround them and provide an Alp like setting. There are old historic camps here and there, but the majority of the shoreline and the land around it is Forever Wild, a designation that means it is land that is New York State owned, and will stay wilderness forever as part of the largest state park in the country, the Adirondack Park. In this way the whole park is protected from development. Any building or renovation project must first be approved by the Adirondack Park Agency, or APA, as well as by local codes offices.

I gratefully reached the opposite side of the lake, and rested my paddle in my lap to take in the scene before me. As I neared the shore I noticed a huge boulder just below the water, probably set in that exact spot centuries ago by the glacial movements that formed these crystal lakes. I thought of how much fun it would be to swim to and stand upon that rock. The water was clear all the way to the stony bottom. I floated in silently, stepped out anxiously and pulled the boat up on shore just enough so it wouldn't slip away.

Stillness abounded. The old camp was set back into the woods a little, but turning back toward the water revealed a magnificent waterfront site. The view across the lake was to nothing but a Forever Wild landscape. It was intoxicating. I could see giant boulders emerging from the opposite shore, way across the lake. There were no visible camps, but I knew there was a wonderfully aged lean-to campsite hidden there, accessible only from the water. A mixture of evergreen and deciduous woods extended as far as the eye could see with silvery birches interspersed to make a lacy pattern. Patches of bright red had begun to appear here and there, the first color of impending fall. Birds skimmed the surface of the waves.

I moved slowly up the hill past an old rickety boathouse that tilted precariously at the water's edge, to explore the building that was nestled into the woods. I could see that many elements of the cabin were in bad condition. The old place was built on concrete block piers, tilted to the side, and looked like a mixture of not very well thought out additions with no apparent views to the lake except from a dark screened porch. As I roamed around the yard and tried to peer in through the small windows, I was delighted with the sight of an old hand built stone fireplace in the tiny living room. It had a small arched fire-box, a stone mantel and stone chimney. I thought about the person who must have lovingly built that old fireplace with his own hands, to keep warm at night in what must have originally been a hunting cabin. At least there was something to save!

I didn't think I could ever afford it on my income, no matter what they were asking. It could never hurt to inquire though, so I called the own-ers from the hand written number on their sign, to ask about their situation and tell them about mine. They were willing to extend owner financ-ing to me as a single mother. Suddenly, possibili-ties began to unfold...

After a year of delay – all the while assuming it would never work, forces came together and I ended up owning the little near-ruin of a place with a spectacular view. Destiny had a plan for me.

The old camp had probably been hand built nearly a hundred years ago by its first owner, without much in the way of carpentry skills, and used in the summers as a retreat. There wasn't a straight plumb wall standing. I don't think he knew for headers, nor cared! Windows and doors were stuck wherever, with just about no structure around them, and no apparent regard for the lake views. Maybe the idea then was just to keep warm from the elements.

To make it livable I had removed a couple of misplaced rooms that had leaked rain like a sieve, and the screened porch, which blocked views from the inside and made the place so dark. It had come with some furniture, but everything was damp and smelly from exposure to the elements for so many years. It took several big dumpsters to get all the rotten or unusable material out, but we got it gutted and prepared to make it a livable summer camp for me and the kids.

Old broken and leaking windows were replaced with new wooden single paned ones, and the original solid wide plank board and batten siding was uncovered, repaired, and re stained. The stone fireplace leaked somewhat, and smoked, but it was the center of attention on cold blustery evenings, so we kept it, and set lots of balsam scented candles on the old stone mantle.

Unfortunately, little mice also enjoyed the fireplace and would scurry up and down the old stones in the evening when things got quiet and we wanted to go to sleep. There was no end to the ways they had found to go in and out of the camp, at will. They were so at home they made us feel like the intruders!

We tore off the aging Masonite paneling that lined the interior walls, and replaced it with fragrant local pine. The ceilings were the exposed wood from the attic floor above. We left the original wood floor, which was fine for camp.

There was a tiny narrow stairs to the attic that was really barely more than a ladder, but there was just enough space up there for a few beds and tables under the eaves. Perfect for the kids and their friends.

The kitchen was gutted and replaced with a rudimentary camp kitchen — in other words, tiny but efficient. One of the best things in the old place was the original kitchen sink, an old porcelain double bowl with a drain board on each side. The twin windows placed above it and a new bridge faucet made it a centerpiece for the little workspace. We added an under counter frig, and a small new stove.

My old camp had been a wonderful place to visit and bring friends for 10 summers, but it sat crookedly on cement blocks, and was inhabitable without heat or insulation in the cold seasons. It was located on a shallow wet spot on the lot, and always felt damp. I had put my log bed in what used to be the living room, by the fireplace, so I would have a view of the lake when I was there. We barely sat inside – we always wanted to be out on the little porch we had built, looking over the lake.

I had very much wanted to save the old place if I could, but it occupied the premier view of the lake, so we would have forever had to use the old tiny spaces to see the water. We wanted to have a family space where we could enjoy the lake all the time. The kids and I had consulted endlessly about it whenever we were up there and finally decided to build a small, but new place, with a sturdy basement foundation. We all wanted something that would last as the family matured and grandkids came, and I wanted to be able to live there all year with heat for the bitterly cold winters.

Building a new house was always more fun because you didn't have to work around old mistakes and dilemmas, dealing with each and every thing that is already there. It was painful too, however, to think of the old camp going away. Emblematic of life, holding on at all cost to what is there — the pain of the ruined marriage, wreck of an affair, or unfulfilling job, seems to be easier because it is better than the agony of uncertainty. Some times you just have to let go and let the new emerge.

I had done projects involving major demolition before though, including the last house I had designed and built for us in Virginia, and knew it would be all right. You just had to get past the emotional day it came down. Then, there would be a whole new world opened with unlimited possibilities – and magnificent views of the lake and the wilderness!

The first time I went to see the camp that spring, no one had driven down the long drive-way all winter, and it was unplowed and snow covered. I was told that was a good thing, because the driveway would have an undisturbed solid frozen base, which would protect it from erosion. On one of those rare dreamlike days where the sun is sparkling bright but big soft snowflakes are drifting down one by one, I walked in on foot. The rushing waters of Wheeler's Creek nearby loudly sang the song of spring yet to come. Rolling white water reeled and crashed down around and through myriad stones and boulders, forming deep swirling pools from the melting snow above. What a fine watering hole for all the creatures that passed through.

The thick woods of pine, cedar, balsam, and birch made the narrow lane we called a driveway seem like a tunneled path. Tracks of deer, fox, coyote, and myriad other smaller animals patterned the snow. It was truly a wonderland, populated by wild creatures who were obviously quite at home and traveled their trails regularly. Tina had told me that when circles of earth started to expose themselves around the bases of the trees, it meant that the bears would be starting to stir, and would soon make their way into the open after a long winter's nap. I was alert to that possibility, but it still seemed early yet. Iona went running up and down exploring everything like it was the first time, even though she had been coming to camp all her life. She seemed so excited to be there and ran up onto the sagging porch to be let in. She must have thought it would be warm inside!

I tentatively stepped onto the slippery porch and pounded the sticking door open with my shoulder. I peered into the kitchen, almost expecting some one to be inside waiting for me.

It was colder in there than outside! It was as still as a tomb, and freezing. Everything looked so cold and empty of life, like a fairy cottage hidden away in the forest, devoid of human habitation for years. I pulled my coat around me closer as I walked through the small rooms and looked at everything, thinking of the many times we had come to stay there as the kids were growing up, and the summers they had spent there while working nearby. There were the sweet memories, but also the heartbreaking ones as they came of age there, with all of those trials, and emotional dramas. We had been through so many experiences, both precious and sorrowful, in the little cabin by the lake.

Through the windows I gazed at the lake beyond. It was pure expanse of white and looked as though you could walk over it for miles and never see a soul. The old giant boulder stood solidly above the surface, with snow covering and drifting over it. I wanted to go take a seat there to take in the view, but didn't dare, with the possibility of the ice thinning. On the far shore, trees leaned from years of wind acting upon them. Spring was about to break, and the air seemed alive with its charge.

It was daunting to think the old place would be gone. Once the process of taking it down began, there would be no turning back, I would have to keep on with it, come what may. It would take a lot of courage to set out on the path of renovating the camp, like renovating my own life. It meant tearing down the old things, the old ways that did not serve me anymore, to allow for the new to emerge. Right down to the very foundations, everything would have to go.

I pulled the heavy door closed behind me and headed slowly back up the driveway in the softening light. My heart was full of emotion as I contemplated the new cycle of my life that was about to begin. No one would blame me if I backed out of this crazy plan and headed back to Virginia. Was I really ready for this dramatic leap into an unknown future? Did I actually have everything it would take to accomplish a complete renovation this place and of my entire life?

Over the next few weeks I gave a couple of old beds away, and with help, stored everything that needed to be saved in the antique dry boathouse that stood crookedly at the lakefront of the camp. Everything that was reusable was kept for the new camp, including the kitchen sink that became the focus of the new camp kitchen design. Light fixtures, plumbing fixtures and fittings, and a fairly new stackable washer/dryer were all part of numerous items that would find a home in the new place. To me, recycling is being green, and it really saves money. Many contractors just find it easier to throw things in the dumpster and start fresh, but to me that's so wasteful. Even the old siding was pried away and taken for re-use on camp outbuildings.

Winter persisted with its cold winds and snow. There were gorgeous sunny days too, when the brilliant sunlight sparkled through the trees and set everything to shimmering and dripping in a kind of anticipation of what was about to come. Those days with the hint of spring lifted my spirit, and inspired me to get going on my construction plans. I was finally listening to my own voice, and I knew what I had to do, but everything ahead would be a new challenge for me now. Everything I thought I had learned would be tested.

Would I be prepared for it?

Each morning I used my quiet time for meditative contemplation, and ideas for the huge task that was before me. I did not question it, but just sat with it, and let all the ramifications flow over me, like water rushing down the creek — taking everything as it came, and going on. Although I did not have a plan in my head, I just felt a pleasant sense of comfort with being with where I was at that moment in time, allowing myself to be led by the positive energy of the cosmos.

There was a quiet, peaceful frame of reference that kept me from feeling worried or concerned about anything. I just knew I was in the right place, and determined to stay right there and let everything evolve as it would. I knew I was about to take a step into my future, without knowing exactly where the path would lead. For the first time in my life, I really didn't need to know. I was ready for anything, with the feeling that a whole new realm was about to open to me.

The words of my teachers rang in my head. "Be in the moment with mindful awareness." It felt like a solid stone anchored into place that I could step to — a strong foundation to build on.

The unfolding of the human heart
is artful and mysterious.
— Jack Kornfield

FIVE

The most important aspect of construction of any new house is the framing. The foundation sets the base, and must be perfect, and then the framing that follows must be of the highest possible quality too so that when it's time for the windows and doors to be set, they will slip into place easily, straight and level. The interior and exterior finishes cannot go into place as they should unless the framing is a proper base.

It was so important to find a great carpentry crew for the framing of the house, and its trim later. Because of the excellent work I had observed of Paul, the contractor who had built the place in which I was staying, I hoped that he would offer a bid for this work. He and his crew were very busy constructing a new boathouse, and he was preparing his workload schedule for the coming season. He had asked for a set of plans to review however, so I was hopeful that he would soon come forward with a bid proposal. He was preoccupied with the work he already had on his roster, but I was determined to get my own project organized and underway. I tried to be patient for an answer, but time was slipping by.

Meanwhile, the other framing contractors I had contacted were not responding either. No one would return my calls. When I did hear from these guys after leaving messages begging them to call me, they each said that they were too busy to take the project. It just didn't make sense that everyone was saying they were too busy in an economy where even I had to leave a business of 25 years behind me, closed for lack of work.

I didn't want to pressure Paul too hard for a concrete bid, because numbers he had casually thrown out to me were way too expensive, but

I was beginning to get desperate for a commitment. Once the demolition took place, the clock would be ticking steadily, and the entire team who would work on the new camp would have to be in place and ready. There would not be much time between when we started, and when the cold of another winter would commence again. Still, I didn't have a framer.

Deciding what to do about Paul's unresponsiveness reminded me of how I had handled things in the past — but this time I would would not hang in there for dear life, adjusting to his needs while waiting for his call. If he wanted the job he would have to take the initiative.

I decided to go back to Virginia and consult with my old framing crew friends to go over the plans with them to see if they would be willing to travel to do the project for me. It was a good possibility because of the downturn in work everywhere.

I left camp and reluctantly headed down the highway for the long trip south, but on my way out of town Paul called on my cell to say, "Hey, don't leave. I want to work with you."

"I want to check and see what my old carpentry friends in Virginia might be willing to do," I told him. "I want to work with you too, if I can, but

I have to know what it will cost. I'll be back in a week, okay?"

Why wouldn't he give me a bid?

While I was in Virginia I visited my family and met with my carpentry friends, but I found that the trip did not provide the answers I was looking for. Even the time I spent in my Virginia house left me feeling empty, and I longed to get back on the road and return to camp.

The kids were away at school. As I wandered through the house I had loved, it had already lost its sense of home for me. I missed the interesting momentum of planning the building project that was already underway for me, and being away from it made me feel like I was wasting time. No one there really understood what I was doing, or why I would ever want to leave my architectural practice and start over. My family and friends just wanted things to stay the way they were, whether I was happy or not.

In my studio, my desk sat cleared off and empty. Everything was neat as a pin — books and files in place, ready for me to start working there again if a call ever came in. I looked at the sunny cheerful room that had always been a joy and comfort to me, but my heart was already in another place.

I gathered some of the things I had been missing, like clothes for the coming warm weather, flip flops, sneakers, and some bathing suits. No one was going to save my dying houseplants, so I grabbed the best of them too and started the long haul back with Iona in the backseat.

When I entered the park it felt so good to be coming back into the north country, which was actually beginning to feel like home! The familiar scent of balsam filled my head as I crossed the "blue line", and I opened the window despite the cold just to breathe it, to feel it pervade my soul.

It would be Easter, the weekend coming up. The lakes were beginning to soften, and water sat smoothly on top of the solid ice, in places. When the sky was clear, the pools reflected it, and now the white frozen lakes were dotted with patches of azure blue. Every now and then the roar of creeks filled the air as the melt-waters rose, rambling down from the mountains.

As for my project, the trip to Virginia had been a bust.

My Virginia friends didn't seem too interested in coming all the way to New York to frame the house for me, though they didn't rule it out either. Once again, I got only vague and noncommittal responses. Now I knew I needed to find someone local, and quickly, since spring was fast approaching.

An important part of doing the project was to gain acceptance and trust from the local contractors, so that they would see for themselves that I was reliable, trustworthy, and knowledgeable…that I did not want to become a competitor for their work. Good relationships with the local contractors would be essential for all of my future work, for I would need their confidence in me for client referrals. I realized that part of their hesitation was because they didn't know me, and couldn't trust that I was capable of running the project myself, and, they didn't want to answer to a woman.

Easter dinner was delightful at Tina's. The food was perfect as always, and her family cheerful and pleasant. Her beautiful home is such a pleasure to be in and speaks of my best work as an architect. It hugs the crest of a thickly wooded hill overlooking a private lake, and spreads out so that every room has a view of the uninterrupted forest and water below. We used dark cove wood siding, a dramatic forest green metal roof, and log posts and trim so that the house blends perfectly into the setting. From the lake, it is invisible, just as we wanted it to be.

In Tina, I had found someone who appreciated the essentially integrated relationship between a home and its setting. As an authentic woodswoman, she wanted her home to reflect her adoration of outdoor life. She and I worked closely on the design, as I always do with clients, so that they are a part of the creative process rather than just recipients of it. A close design partnership throughout all the phases of the architectural work allows the client to be able to review, understand, and make changes to the work as it proceeds, so that the end result is something they have created together with the architect, as a team.

Tina's camp is light filled space that intermingles with its wooded setting. Porches and gardens are only a step away off every main room. It glows with her own interior design, the elegance of a Great Camp with a soft feminine touch that includes a magnificent collection of Adirondack antiques, artwork, furs, and silver. A huge moose head trophy that looks as if it is still breathing dominates the gorgeous lodge room in the center, where French doors and a wall of glass with transom windows brings light into the depths of the space, and a panoramic view of the lake beyond. Every room reflects her caring attention to detail.

Over the long table while we enjoyed dinner, Tina's family and guests all sympathized with my difficulties getting people to return calls or commit to anything. They nodded in agreement when I told them about my fears of being a source of competition for the men who had worked locally all of their lives and didn't want an outsider coming in and thinking they knew what they were doing. They cheerfully shared the names of carpenters they knew and had worked with, who they thought might be more open to joining my project. I went home from the wonderful evening with a list of people to call in the morning, all with high recommendations.

The next morning before I could make any calls, however, Paul called to ask if I could meet him over at my old camp so he could talk to me and show me some things. I was pleased that he had caught me before I had started searching for someone else. Maybe there was still some hope that we could work together. I tried to keep calm but I was excited.

We were able to drive down the melting driveway, but it was bitter cold even in the sun. Paul moved about the old place knowingly and pointed out trees that should come down, things in the old camp that he thought should be saved and the ways he determined to proceed. It was obvious that he had looked things over here and thought about what he wanted to do. I had lots of ideas of my own but I listened patiently so I could learn more about him, and the way he worked.

I followed as he walked down toward the lake, and as he stepped through the woods he named a price for the framing. It was less than I had expected from him because of the higher numbers he had casually indicated to me previously. He had a great reputation in the area, had built many lakefront custom camps, and was particularly known for those where his craftsmanship with log construction could be showcased. I had been afraid that I would have to negotiate with him until we could arrive at something I could live with, but he was already there with his reasonable offer.

We agreed on it, and I told him I was really happy – that he had been my first choice all along. I sincerely knew in my heart that we would become good friends and have fun working together. I told him just that. He looked doubtful, but shook my hand when I held it out to him. I was so delighted at that moment because somehow I knew it was right. A new alliance had been created.

With that handshake I committed myself to start on a new, exciting path into the future of my life. Did I have a strong enough foundation to embark on this journey to an unknown place? It meant a new building project far away from the old friends I had always worked with, closing my practice that I had developed for years — starting over in a new place, as an unknown. I can't say that I was unafraid, but I was most surely excited! My heart was bursting with the joy that this thing was beginning to reveal itself, and I was on my way.

I started to put my team of subcontractors together. Now that I had the main piece of the puzzle, the framing, all the other parts began to fall into place.

When I told Tina about the big news of getting ready to begin the construction, of course she was hesitant, skeptical. How could I be so sure that everything was going to work out? Didn't I need someone to step in and consult with – someone who knew the ins and outs of the region? She listened to my responses with patience, without judgment. I wasn't always sure she had total confidence in me, but things were coming together in just the right way, without undo effort, so I braced myself with determination.

There was something deeper, too. A sense of knowing had grown stronger. It was as if the cosmos was working in step behind me, leading me to the correct answers that would bring me to where I needed to be. Still, it was definitely a leap of faith – a dive into the enticing waters of renewal. The first small changes in my inner life were starting to change what happened in my outer world. I was beginning to understand what it felt like to be truly at home.

The first major endeavor was to get the demolition of the old camp done, so that excavation could occur for the new foundation. I had several offers for this work but one stood way out from the others because one contractor, Bob K, was willing to do everything – the demo, debris removal, the excavation, taking down necessary trees, installing the footings, foundation and slab, and even providing the new septic field and work on the driveway. This offer was attractive in so many ways because the price was fair, and the coordination would just be between the two of us, not with several people each with a gigantic truck to find room for on my narrow lot. I decided to go with him and asked him to come and start the demo work as soon as he was able to.

Meanwhile Paul's crew cut out the old electrical panel and put in a temporary on a nearby tree for our use during the construction period. They were able to save the phone line too, so we could have a line at the site at all times. They disconnected and removed all appliances, plumbing fixtures, lights, cabinets, and everything that we could save, carting it out to the boathouse where it would be stored. Even the windows and doors were saved for other renovations people might need them for. It was so cold in the old camp on the days they worked, clearing it out, that I could hardly stand to be there. It was as if the inside of the camp took in and retained the cold, while the early spring sun began to warm the earth outside.

On the day of demolition I was there bright and early so I could watch the whole thing. Bob was in his big tractor already, beginning the job. The tractor would approach the building, and seem to take a great big bite out of it, and spit it out into the huge dump truck to be taken away. It was fascinating, but at times I turned away so that I would not have to look too closely at everything coming apart. The maw of the tractor opened wide and big sharp teeth bit into the cabin and tore pieces away like a lioness feeding on her kill.

In just a few hours the cabin was completely gone. There was a large empty space where it had been, and that would become the site of the new house. The spot was cleaned of all debris, level and smoothed.

I walked around and took in the raw feeling of the land and the way it began to relate in new ways to the water and the woods all around it. Without the cabin, it felt so expansive, so clear and ready for all the creative possibilities I could ever think of. It was a big step to take all the old used parts of my life away and prepare for all that would be new.

I felt emotional as I saw the parallel between the renovation of this house and the renovation of my entire life. The old had been stripped away.

My old practice was gone, the Virginia house was for sale, the kids were gone and the camp was gone too.

Now, there was a clear open space for everything that was to come. I could feel some fear in the process, but I knew too that uncertainty was always accompanied by fear. And what is fear? The opposite of love. I knew I had to acknowledge the fear, allow myself to feel it, and let it go, transforming it into love for myself, my beautiful life, my family and the precious people who had come to me for this exciting creative endeavor. Everything would be as it should be. To trust in love takes an enduring courage. Did I have that kind of courage? Could I make this huge leap of faith and plunge into a completely different kind of life?

The bright sun warmed my head as I quietly walked in meditation down toward the lake. I saw the old boulder standing tall, steadfast and almost completely out of the icy lake, awaiting the rise of spring, just as I was. As I identified with its strength, I felt the emergence of my heart's desire. A profound feeling of joy entered my chest as a spreading warmth that traveled to the top of my head, and to the tips of my toes. My steps lightened, and a small smile came to my face. My entire body was expressing its answer, "Yes!"

A few days later when we met again at the site to begin the foundation, it snowed. I stood at the edge of the woods beneath its sheltering boughs with the snow swirling all around and watched the big tractor scoop cold dirt to make the hole. I wondered if the crew would quit because of the snow and go home, but they looked at me quizzically when I asked that question, as if I was crazy. I had no choice but to bundle up further and stand my ground if I wanted to see this amazing part of the work. So I did — I went for my heavy mittens and a thick scarf that were still in the car, and returned to observe the process.

The ground was still frozen as the big machine bit into it. White frozen flecks of ice permeated the hard cold earth in the deepest parts, and freezing cold water drained into the hole from the higher spots uphill. I wondered how we would ever get this big hole dry enough to set and pour footings, but Bob was unconcerned. He was used to all these things as part of spring construction in the Adirondacks. Besides, he had to start his projects early in the year so he could be done with all his work for hunting season every fall! All day the huge tractor dug into the rough earth, and cut the hole as neatly as if with a bread knife slicing a fresh loaf.

The next morning was still bitterly cold when I arrived at the big hole, expecting it to be entirely filled with water. Surprisingly it was fairly dry, the men had already laid down gravel and were staking the forms for the footings. These people wasted no time whatsoever. Once the footings were inspected, they were poured and we were ready for walls.

Next the crew set up forms for the concrete walls of the basement. They even raced each other starting from one corner to see who would get to the finishing corner first. I loved the atmosphere of humor and professionalism that characterized their work. The younger men teased their boss (and father) for talking with me so much that he would surely lose the race this time, but with all our chatting he still made it to the finish just before the younger ones.

Of course he had the advantage of telling them to keep going back to check to their work! I never in all my experience had seen a crew check dimensions and diagonals as many times as they did. They were precise. Any builder knows that a perfectly squared foundation is critical to the framing of the house.

Extreme care and precision at this phase would set the stage for the skillful installation of all that would follow.

Every day, as work progressed, I came to observe everything that was happening. Concrete walls were poured to support the house. My new camp! I felt rejuvenated!

Spring was energetically trying to make its appearance, but the days were still cold and I had to keep moving while I was watching the work. There was plenty of cleaning up to do around the property, so I rebuilt the old campfire pit out by the lake and brought the debris there to burn. It was so beautiful standing at the crackling campfire and looking out onto the melting ice and encroaching water, watching the arrival of spring wildlife onto the scene. The loons would arrive as soon as they could make a water landing.

Slowly but surely each day, the rising lake made the great boulder just offshore seem to sink gently down into the water where it rested on its solid stone base and would anchor our cove, forever. With the ice going out, it wouldn't be long before it was completely submerged again in rising waters, but we would always know it was there.

There was plenty of time to think as I worked. Again it occurred to me how this project reflected the progression of my own life. This time, the footings and foundation were as strong and grounded as they possibly could be. There was no overlooking of problems or defects, no excuses for accepting the unacceptable, no mistakes permitted. This time I was determined to build my life around something that was solid, which came from my own inner strength and vision, not what some one else wanted me to have. I was creating the foundations of a life that would be solidly anchored, to support my growth and wellbeing for all the days going forward.

Before I knew it, the basement slab was in place, the concrete walls stripped of their forms and Paul's framing crew had arrived. The first floor was under construction. Sure as Bob had promised, the basement was dry. I couldn't believe it.

Again, I never saw so much measuring and checking. Every board that was put into place was checked for level and accuracy. The crew was cheerful but hardworking. They had a routine for sure, arriving promptly in the morning, taking a short 30 minute lunch break in their trucks or out by the water, then continuing on for the afternoon. They weren't even allowed to listen to a radio, because Paul did not want rock and roll to tarnish the peacefulness of the wilderness all around us. This rule truly did increase the feeling of respect and reverence for where we all were, doing our work, bringing a new place to life in this precious place.

The early birds of spring were arriving, chirping their encouragement, and my spirits continued to rise each day that I heard their songs intermingled with the sounds of hammering, and the popping of the nail gun.

It was beginning to be black fly season, and I asked the crew if they would have to take a break for that. Again, they looked at me like I was from a distant planet, but said kindly, "no, we're used to it…"

I wasn't. This was the first spring I had spent in the Adirondacks, and I had to take up arms against the troublesome insects. It felt like they wanted to drive humans away at any cost! They would light on you and take a bite without your even realizing it till your hand would snap up to smack them and come back bloody. The crew had welts on them and blood dripping down their necks, though it didn't seem to bother them despite how badly they looked. I tried the locally made salves because I couldn't bear to spray myself with the toxic sprays that didn't seem to work anyway. The only real solution was to keep every part of your body covered, hair and head to toe.

It occurred to me that even in the place of your brightest dreams — nothing was going to be perfect.

When the first deck was complete I was so excited, as I always was at this stage of work. At last I could climb up and walk around on the sweet smelling platform to see the world from the perspective of the new house, and the actual views that would be visible from all the rooms from windows yet to come. When everyone was gone for the day I sat alone on the new first floor and took in the feeling of expansiveness.

The beauty of the setting amazed me. Everything I could see across the lake was Forever Wild, so there were no camps, houses or other buildings, and none could ever be built there.

This was the environment that would be part of the new house – although it was the outdoors, it would be integral to the inside too. The spirit of the new house would fix itself on this site, opening to it, and the essence of the site would become the heart of the home.

There were a few old lean-tos and water accessible campsites in the distance, but they were hidden within the woods. Next door on one side there was a camp with a boathouse, but all the shoreline camps beyond it were blocked from my view by that boathouse. On the other side, all I could see was wild woods, and the spectacular lake beyond it through the woods. The far shore was alive with the fresh green of spring, and the azure lake was gently moving. I could always foretell what sort of weather was coming, by looking at the lake. It would be as reflective as a mirror, or churning with white-caps.

My entire being was filled with happiness. I couldn't stop smiling to myself. I had been blessed with this beautiful place, and a new home was emerging for me right here in the place I had dreamed of, and it was right. The cosmic forces that were leading me had brought me to this very place, at this perfect time, and I could feel harmony in my heart.

The next step was to build the walls on the deck, with their window and door openings in place. These openings would frame the wilderness views and bring all their majesty into the house. The house would be filled with the scents, sounds, scenes and the light of the wild.

As the walls were built on deck and raised up, the structure of the house began to take shape. We worked together on the framing of the important window walls, which I wanted done in a particular way so that the windows would have a certain separation from each other for their future trimming, and that they would all be exactly the same, and all perfectly centered in their spaces. This was not a typical job where the plans could be used as a general guide, and things placed sort of the way they were drawn. A bit of insistence on perfection now would make for the symmetry later that I believe makes for great design.

Further, my respect for skilled carpentry is such that I abhor asking anyone who has built something with care, to rip it out for any reason. It really helps in every way to give maximum attention to the project at each step, before the work is done, so that it can be done correctly the first, and only, time.

During framing, every day feels like Christmas. There is a new gift of space that happens almost constantly. And, you can still feel the presence of the world around you all the time. You are not cut off from it, but a part of it. The house is both the inside and outside at the same time. Shelter embraces but does not confine you. I always dread the day when sheathing, siding and roofing begin to enclose the house and the dreamlike feeling it has during framing dissipates.

With Paul and his crew there was never anger or complaining. A sense of humor was always in the air. The men willingly listened to my requests and interjected their own ideas, which were almost always helpful. Listening to them was as important to me as them hearing me out, because I wanted us to work together and have fun doing it. I wanted them to walk away when the job was done remembering the good experience they had while they were on my project. I had the feeling that Paul had only assigned people to my project who got along with each other, because they were so unusually happy. Maybe it was the quiet...

Demonstrating gratefulness to the crew, rather than ordering them around so they know who's boss, is essential for mutual respect and seamless teamwork. I truly did feel so blessed and thankful for all the men were doing, and for the skillful way they carried out their work.

By now I felt such deep gratitude in my soul — for being led to come here — for this gratifying project, and for what was apparently going to be the start of a new life. It was spilling out of me. I made a point to thank them at the end of each day for their work, and I was so glad to see them arrive again the next day smiling.

There comes a day in very early spring when the water calls to you. The freezing chill of stepping into it goes straight to the bone, but the soothing warmth of the sun on your face, and the promise of what's out there waiting for you, are irresistible. One clear and sunny morning, that call came.

I dragged my old red kayak out of the boathouse and carried it down to the shoreline with my paddle and life jacket. A tentative step into the water brought me to the boat and I sat down into the familiar black seat with a gentle push out onto the lake. I let the boat just float gently there, in the silence.

Then I cut the sharp edge of the black graphite paddle into the transparent solidity of the perfectly still water, on the in breath. There was a pause as I looked up into the wild beyond and wondered what would be out there just for me in that seemingly perfect moment. On my outbreath a soft sigh escaped me – and with it the thought, ahhhh. Like sliding into silky sheets on a summer evening, I slid as one with my boat into the silent, cold, crystal clear water. The light sparkling drip from the paddle was the only sound.

Settling into the narrow boat I leaned back to feel the wide expanse of the endless blue sky above. There was no need to paddle, for the kayak glides forth on it's own, knowing it's lake home so well. As the sun closed my eyes in the glory of this unimaginable solitude, a silent floating meditation pervaded my soul.

I was alone, but not totally alone. There was no one at the lakeside camps yet. The summer people were waiting for school to get out and the black flies to have gone. But there was a quiet activity out there beyond and I became curious. Had the loons arrived to reclaim and refurbish their old nest? Was the magical great heron watching from his usual hiding places on the shore? Was the old creek spilling its bubbling spring waters over the rocks into the cove? All these questions invited me into the mode of a gentle exploration – an investigation of what would be new, and what was the same.

For that moment, the lake was all mine, and all it's inhabitants my own intimate family. The loon pair would let me into their private nesting routine, because they knew I was safe with their secrets. They knew I would count the days till their tiny chicks burst forth into the world, and take their first swim in celebration of their birth. And from that very moment, they too would belong to me for the summer.

The minutes flew by and I had no idea how long I'd been gone. I felt at one with the world. The sounds and smells, the sun and the water were my universe.

The floating world.
Everything in life is like cargo on a fragile boat,
a skiff on the wide water of our transient life.
Awakening is a willingness to take each step,
without knowing where the path leads,
and allowing whatever unfolds to prompt the next step.

SIX

As the house and the beginnings of summer progressed, I knew I would have to find a place to stay when the owners of the camp I was temporarily in would come take it over for their summer. One afternoon when there was not much I could do as the crew worked, I decided to go explore and clean out the upper floor of the old boathouse that sat on the edge of the lake. It's not in the water, so it is called a dry boathouse. However, beneath it there is always water. It drains down from the higher levels of the property and the mountains beyond it, through a depression beneath the building. It had been jacked up and leveled several times over the years, but it would always sink back into it's own position, which was tilted to the East, and stay there.

Underneath it are two huge long logs, one on each side that form the support for the first floor, so these may have been skids which brought the structure over ice to its resting place by the lake.

The boathouse is made entirely of logs and pine boards, and has an open room on the first floor, which we were using for the storage of kayaks, the canoe, and currently for all the saved materials from the old cabin. There was another empty room above under the eaves of the roof. I was told that the original owner made it his art studio, on the water's edge, and I could always imagine the idea of his having a place to paint and draw right over the water — how nice that would have been.

Two tall multi-paned windows that span from eye level to the floor made it feel like you were floating right over the water, as you looked out from up there. When the window panels were raised back and up toward the ceiling and clamped open, the cool breeze and sounds from the lake came right into the room. Some one had strategically placed a handrail at each opening to prevent one from falling down a story into the lake.

The attic room was filled with old lengths of wood, leftover shingles from roof repairs over the years, but fortunately no trash. I threw these down to the ground from the upper landing of the wooden stair that led to the second level. The dry wood would be perfect for campfires. As I swept the place clean, breathing in the pungent smell of very old things, I began to take in the ancient charm of the place, and it hit me that this was going to be my summer home!

I got that place swept clean as a whistle. I brushed off the peeled log rafters that framed the roof and the pine decking of the ceiling. The roof sloped down to a 3' high knee wall along each of the long sides to form the room. Two large gables shaped the end walls — one faced the new house, with a solid wood entrance door and the original stairway coming up from the ground, and in the other gable was a magnificent view of the lake through the two tall multi-paned windows, many of the panes broken. Immediately I could imagine my mattress placed right in front of the window openings so I could see the water from bed. It would be like living and sleeping in a floating world.

I brought a cotton dhurrie rug up from the storeroom below, and asked the crew to bring my stored mattress up into the space too. Paul became alarmed when he heard of my plans and forbid me from going up and down the rickety stairs until he could get them stabilized. Next thing I knew there were braces on the ancient steps and a new wooden platform landing at the bottom to transverse the wet soggy grass that led to the bottom of the stairs.

The crew unhinged the two huge windows and brought them up into the unfinished new house for me, setting them on sawhorses so that I could attack the re-glazing of the broken windowpanes. It would be important to be able to close them from the bugs and the weather if I were to get a comfortable night's sleep out there. I took a count of the cut glass and other materials I would need. I was delighted to think of spending time working in the lakefront space that would soon become the living room of the new house. The crew was working steadily in there, installing windows and doors, continuing with the interior framing.

From my vantage point in the upper boathouse I would watch the house emerge on the wooded lot behind me. While a house I had designed was under construction sometimes a client would ask, "Is this what you expected the house to be like?"

Many of them could not envision what their structure would look like before it was built and they could actually see it. They could not really see the three dimensional building while it was still on paper. I could certainly understand that, but for me it's there before the first line is drawn.

I had read years ago that Frank Lloyd Wright told his apprentices that he would dream a vision of the entire house he was about to design before he set down the first line of drawing. He wanted his apprentices to be able to do that. At first I couldn't imagine possessing such a skill, but as time went by I found that I could actually do it. Then I found that it was a practice that I was doing regularly. I loved this super ability that he so inspired me with, to dream, and then to draw.

Among the trees, my house was emerging from dreams to reality right before me. The boathouse windows needed work, and it wouldn't be a dream sleeping there if I could not close the windows when the mosquitoes came out. I wasn't thinking much about mosquitoes though, I just enjoyed working on the old window panels in the open space with the crew every day. I looked forward to their lunch breaks and planned my own so that I could listen to them during their short time off to relax. They got so used to me that sometimes they forgot I was there. That was great for me because then they would talk in their normal ways without having to try to be ever so polite. I was one of them but they always saw me as the owner and were on their guard, especially because of the restrictions Paul had made for behavior on the job. Every man was always a gentleman.

As I started on the window glazing job I had no idea what I was doing, having never done it before. The big windows were set out in the emerging living room for me, and all the materials were there. I started scraping out the flaking chalky grout, which was disintegrating and falling out around each pane. It turned out to be a much bigger project than I had anticipated, because every single pane needed re-grouting, not just the ones with broken or missing glass. The ancient grout was just too old to do its job anymore.

As time went by I discovered what I needed to know. The crew brought me better tools than I had, having done this before. It was meticulous work but rewarding, as each new piece of glass could be placed into the scraped and bare place, secured, grouted with fresh soft material and cleaned. Then the whole panel of panes needed cleaning again, on each side.

One day when Paul came in for his regular visit he said, "I had no idea you could do this kind of work…" and I just had to reply, "neither did I." As with many things in life, you never know till you've tried.

After the work was completed, the grout had to set up, so the windows could not be put back into place before it was time for me to move into the boathouse. The two big openings were bare, bringing the lake right into the space. It felt like literally floating right over the water.

Meanwhile we moved the little refrigerator from the old camp up from storage, with an enamel topped table that would be "the kitchen". There would be no cook top, so I bought an electric teakettle from the local hardware store. Hot

tea in the mornings would just about make anything else bearable, food wise. I added an old
table desk and a few chairs and rockers. I made up
the bed with lots of pillows, warm flannel bedding
and a quilt, though it was summer, because the
nights were always cool, especially on the water.
In place of a bathroom, there were an enamel
washbasin and potty.

When the fourth of July weekend approached
I had to get out of camp Omega for good. There
was not much to pack because I had not brought
much to begin with. I gathered all my belongings into the car before I cleaned and readied
the camp for the owners to come and enjoy their
wonderful place for the summer.

The day was dripping with rain and more
rain kept coming. I drove to my camp and lugged
everything from the car across the long grassy
yard and up the steps into the boathouse. A quick
flip of the old light switch revealed no power, so
I was disappointed that there was not going to be
any electricity on my first night, although it was
planned for connection to the new panel later.
When I finished hauling my things from the car
I decided to go out again before the weather got
worse and darkness fell, to get a battery powered
lantern that would at least give me some sense of

security for the night. I had no idea what my time in this camp would be like, but I was trusting that I would adjust to it and it would be fine. Just like in the old days when people to the Adirondacks without much in the way of conveniences, like kitchens and bathrooms.

I came back to the camp with my new lantern and placed it beside the bed. With some candles on the table for when it got dark I felt pretty good, but not nearly as good as when I saw Paul come walking toward the lake from the driveway. The rain had let up but everything was still soaking wet. He was in a good mood, eating an ice cream cone, which he called his dinner. He brought his tools out of his truck and I soon realized that he was prepared to stay there until he had connected electricity from the temporary panel near the house, to boathouse. What a beautiful surprise!

As he worked, I tried to help, we talked, and laughed – had fun. This was something that was not a part of his job responsibility in framing the house for me, but I was so grateful that he had remembered this would be my first night out here alone. To have electricity for the little place, a light at the door and power for the refrigerator, lamps and a radio working inside made my place a tiny home.

When he left I felt very alone again. The stillness of the woods and the gentle lapping of the water against the rocky shore just added to the sense of isolation. Iona looked at me and tilted her head as if to ask, "What are we doing here?" She was probably wondering when we would be heading back to the car and home.

At least there was light from the little lamps and the comfort of some of my own belongings to provide a sense of familiarity. I pulled the heavy wooden door closed with a sigh and looked around in the soft yellow light. My books and journal were at my bedside, the carved animals I had been working on stood on the long low knee wall beside a few porcelain birds and real nests I had collected, and candles were flickering on the table. Some clothes hung on hangers from the rafters with my boating hat balanced above them, the rest folded in stacks on an old plank table.

Long old nails were a perfect way to hang towels, baskets filled with brushes and toiletries, and the hair dryer. Food was carefully stowed in snap shut glass canisters and mason jars away from the nighttime escapades of mice. There was an antique fabric sling rocking chair with a footstool. The bed was made with red plaid flannel sheets and a log cabin quilt. It sure looked sweet and cozy.

I was glad to have the solidity of the wooden door between me and the forest, because a pair of bears had been wandering along the shoreline from camp to camp in the past few weeks, and I was ever so grateful I wasn't going to go to sleep in a tent! They could climb the stairs of course, but just might be deterred by the racket Iona was bound to make if she heard anyone or anything approaching.

I crawled into the warmth of the soft cotton flannel, turned out the light and lay there quietly while the cool breeze from the lake drifted over my face.

Mixed with the musty scent of old pine-wood inside was the fertile fragrance of balsam woods and fresh water all around me. In the distance, the loons called to each other in all their many voices. I listened to the wildness of their songs and knew that I was truly, at that moment, an integral part of it. The light of the moon reflected softly over the lake, and soon everything seemed illuminated with a magical glow. I said a prayer of gratitude and asked for the protective guidance of the guardian angels and spirits that I knew were always with me, and went to sleep that night in a gentle peace.

The next morning the lake was a buzz with fourth of July weekend activity. As I laid there listening to the commotion I remembered how wonderful it was when I was a kid to be the first one out in the morning on the smooth flat lake on water skis, so I couldn't blame those out there already blasting my serenity with loud motor boats and jet skis. This just wasn't going to be a place where one could "sleep in". Leaning up on my elbow I could see the whole lake from bed. A beautiful day was dawning.

I looked over at my new house under construction admiringly as I brushed my teeth out on the stair landing and spit into the grass below. Water for tea boiled in a matter of moments and I silently praised the ingenuity of the electric tea-pot. Just like home, I slipped back under the covers with the mug steaming at the bedside and took some time to gather my thoughts and do some inspirational reading and meditation, to start my day.

The day was all mine.

I remembered the way I had felt back in Virginia — like I was trying to fit into clothes that didn't belong to me. How things had shifted.

I felt like my life was opening up like my favorite flowers, the sweet white water lilies that floated in the quiet coves. They reminded me of the lotus blossom, and all its promise as a symbol of the open heart.

Midmorning, Tina pulled up to the floating dock with her family motorboat and tooted the horn. I leaned out over the water to greet her.

"Want to go for a boat ride?" she asked.

No need to think that over. I grabbed my hat and scrambled onto the dock and into the boat. She wanted to explore the whole lake to see which summer friends were "in" (camp) and hear all the news. We took off and sped down the lake to find out what was happening at each of the old places, and see the familiar folks she had spent summers with all her life.

One of the neighbors across the lake always grilled free hot dogs out in his lakefront yard for everybody who stopped at his dock on the fourth, so we didn't hesitate to take advantage of that for an outdoor lunch and visit. I met so many people, all of them happy to see the beginning of another summer. Tina told each of them about my new place being built on the lake, and they all said they'd be by in their boats to see it. The whole day was just delightful, the air so fresh and the sun bright and warm.

As we pulled up beside my dock in late afternoon I realized I should have used sunblock – my face was warm and pink, but it felt good. I thanked Tina profusely for taking me on such a great adventure of a day, and headed for the boat-house as she backed carefully out of the cove and motored down to her family camp. Something looked different as I looked up at the boathouse, but I couldn't quite figure – there were screens on the big window openings! What good fairy had blessed me with those?

I climbed the stairs and creaked open the wood door and peered at them. I couldn't believe my eyes. Someone had come and carefully measured those big openings, built wooden screen panels to exactly fit, and installed them on the outside of the building so that the windows could still fit perfectly into the openings when we could put them back up, to be drawn back and clamped open. It would have required a ladder rising up a full story to do that work from the ground lakeside.

I knew it was Paul. He had come and done this without even telling me, knowing that I would be bitten alive if I didn't have protection from the bugs all summer. No one that I could think of had ever given me a gift like this one – something I really needed, didn't ask for, that took so much effort and work, and on a holiday weekend. I sat down and looked through the beautiful new screens at the lake beyond, and felt amazed and so very touched. This was a very special man indeed.

A few nights later as I was getting ready for bed, a huge rainstorm began to come across the lake. Dark gray clouds were gathering, and wind was gusting across the water, blowing into the boathouse. The windows were still resting on the sawhorses over at the new house, the grout setting up. Although there was a wide roof overhang facing the lake, I knew that strong winds and rain were going to come right into the place and could soak everything, including me.

I quickly pulled my bed away from the windows as far as I could and looked around for something to cover the openings with. There was nothing waterproof around. I would have to use some of my cotton blankets, the only thing large enough to cover the wide expanse open to the oncoming storm. I tacked them to the top and even hung some over the inside of the handrails for the lower parts. I put extra cotton blankets on my bed to cover the quilt and bedding. The howling wind was beginning to get scary.

When there was nothing else left to do, I got into the bed and listened apprehensively to the storm rage as it came across the water. This couldn't last forever, I thought. It would be over before long and if I could just go to sleep I would wake up to calmer weather. That proved to be impossible. I lay there listening and startling to cracks of thunder and lightning. The rain poured down loudly and the wind howled. Iona looked at me with questioning eyes, "Why can't we get out of here?"

The blankets at the window openings were getting soaked and heavy with wetness, and the cover over my bed was even getting wet. It seemed like the blowing wind and rain would never end. What in the world was I doing out here in this place anyway? Had I lost my mind? My family was astonished and worried that I would chose to stay out here in the boathouse for the summer, but till now I had thought the solution was perfect. Now I had my doubts.

It was a hellish long night, but finally the storm began to quiet, and I fell asleep in the cold chilly wet out of sheer exhaustion. Mother Nature had thrown everything she had at me and somehow I had passed her test of endurance!

The next morning the sun came out and with it the backbreaking chore of hanging all those blankets to dry. Fortunately the rain did not penetrate my actual bed, so once I had everything hung out all over the place, I could relax knowing I would be able to sleep comfortably that night. I had managed the worst the weather could show me, now all I had to face was the heat of summer, and the bears!

When the grout was finally set, we re-hung the big windows in the boathouse, and I clamped them up to the rafters so the maximum breeze could come through from the lake. The days were getting hotter. Fortunately, every night brought cool breezes, eventually. I was getting accustomed to being there, and when neighbors and friends found out where I was living they generously offered me the use of their bathrooms and showers. I swam in the lake in the late afternoons, and washed up mornings from the basin with lake water, but a nice indoor hot shower was something to cherish. Every time I climbed the stairs I made sure I carried a pitcher of water from the lake, for tea, dishwashing and cleaning up.

I kept my meals simple, cereal and fruit, salads, fresh vegetables, humus, and tuna salad with tomato were staples of my diet every day. Surprisingly, I did not get bored with the limitation of not being able to cook. It was refreshing!

Sometimes visitors would call to me from their kayaks or canoes, which could easily float right up to the boathouse in the water below. Some were friends I knew and others were curious neighbors from around the lake. It was just like living in a marina where you might keep your houseboat in a slip, with nothing but boats and water around you. My floating world was as fascinating as it was unique. There were the quiet times of dawn and dusk, but also the friendly animated atmosphere of a relaxed summer community of folks who just love to be on the lake.

My grown kids had arrived for the summer, had found a variety of jobs locally, and a place to stay in a friend's camp at a nearby lake. My daughter would run the four miles from over there to our dock, take a swim and have a visit with me, then run back or get a lift from me if she was too tired to make the round trip. We would sit up at the future screened porch of the new house, where we could enjoy the view and be in the cool shade. I loved to listen to all the news and daily happenings in my kid's lives, knowing the summer would fly by and they would soon be gone again. This was going to be our permanent home now, and it would be further than ever from them when they returned to school, about twelve driving hours away at Virginia Tech.

In my efforts to do everything I could possibly do on the house myself, I set up a staining center right beside the house, and rolled/brushed on a semi clear light stain on every single piece of siding and trim that would be installed on the house. I wanted the wood to retain its natural color, but also to protect it from moisture and mold formation. The exterior of the windows had been ordered a natural shade that I hoped the siding would become when it aged. The idea of this combination was taken from the oldest camps in the region, which were built with local materials and allowed to weather naturally for years.

It was fairly easy work but took many hours and many days to get through all that material. The crew lifted pieces from my drying area to apply to the house. The house was looking really beautiful with all the natural cedar and pine as its skin. A dark bronze metal roof topped it off so graciously.

I wanted everything to be natural and real in this house of wood, stone and glass. To enter the structure was to feel the magical affect it could have on anyone who came to see it — the sense of peace and belonging it brought to ones very being. It had begun to blend into its setting and was a part of it. The design and materials were a reflection of my life at this moment – a return to what is honest and true, my spiritual home. From every interior space there was a connection to the exterior world – the deep expanse of the woods and the lake, and the bright eastern morning sun that entered and traveled through the house as the day progressed, bringing light and warmth but also new life with each new day.

All summer I lived on site and worked building the house. It was a joyous task that is indescribable. Each day another piece would come to life as the puzzle came together.

My own heart was coming to life too. Nothing could hold me back from participating in a the heartfelt energy that had been obscured for so long, like a shining jewel covered in dust. I knew instinctively that this precious force had been working within me all along, and was moving me into the exactly right place I needed to be. It was such a wonderful time, to be free to be doing exactly what I was happy to be doing and it see it evolve so beautifully. How different this was than all the times when I had felt compelled to do what everyone else needed, as I stifled my own joyous spirit. Everything was resonating, "Welcome to the world of the real you!"

I was so pleased to be a part of creating something so fitting to the woods and the lake. The house was modest, but its spaces felt sacred and elegant in their reverence for the wilderness site. I knew that the inner glow that I felt showed all over my face, like a light that was at last revealing itself, and it felt so good to be truly happy.

You must learn one thing.
The world was meant to be free in.
Give up all the other worlds
except the one in which you belong.
Sweet Darkness, The House of My Belonging
— David Whyte

SEVEN

The entire time I had been in the Adirondacks I had not received a single call for architectural work. The situation was somewhat amazing, if not terrifying. Here I was, in the midst of an emerging new life, and at the same time facing an income draught.

The house in Virginia was on the market, but the phone and voice mail were still connected and I checked regularly to see if I'd had any interview requests. There were absolutely none.

The truth was, though I needed income and wanted work, I was also grateful to have been given the time to focus all my attention on building my house and creating the next steps in my life. On the other hand, I had to survive. I took some small jobs like camp cleaning, to make ends meet. For about $150, I would work all day, cleaning away mouse droppings and the occasional dead bird, clearing off a layer of winter dust on everything, cleaning the kitchen thoroughly and scouring the bathrooms, then vacuuming the entire camp, which would be exhausting. It really made me contemplate the idea that I had been designing beautiful homes for years, and now I was reduced to cleaning them. There's nothing like spending time with a vacuum cleaner to make you think, especially about troubling things.

There was no work in Virginia, but there was nothing coming in for me here in the north country either. I certainly didn't want to take up camp cleaning as a second career, and even if I did, it was seasonal! What would bring in a living for the long winters I knew were coming? I still had another year and a half of college expenses too, before both kids would be done.

I knew that the proceeds of the sale of the house in Virginia would be a help, but those funds had always been designated as "retirement", because I had no pension or any other incoming money other than social security to look towards. I didn't want to spend every last cent I had just to live day to day.

I took the risk of spending even more money and placed an ad in the local weekly newspaper to appear every week for the entire season. It was scary to be spending more instead of earning what I really needed, but it was the only way I could really let it be known that I had arrived here to stay, and was ready to take in work. It would be necessary for my name to be recognizable – for people to get used to seeing my logo in the paper every week until it became familiar – and recognize my local number and address right around the corner.

What I had been learning for some time now was this: It is incredibly important to take the right view of things.

I couldn't help but feel that there was a cosmic plan in place that had brought me through many trials, emotional and financial, to this very place in time. All the forces had come into alignment for me to receive the message to come to the Adirondacks, and when I got here, to go ahead and do this project, leave the past behind me and enter into a new time of my life. An old cycle was ending; the new one had begun. All I had to do was believe, and keep going forward, following the signs. The I Ching likens it to a stream flowing on, around rocks and into and out of holes and depressions, flowing on to where it is destined to go, adapting to what comes, unafraid and persevering.

One thing I had learned in my many struggles was that if one is on the right path, it will be easy. Of course there will be stumbling blocks, but generally not major obstructions. If things just never seemed to go right, everything always a big trial, then my direction was off, and I needed to rethink and regain my balance. When I allowed myself to be led, my mind would be open to all things, and accordingly, I would be flexible and adaptable. If I made mindfulness my way of being, I would be able to feel or hear the messages being given to me. Alternatively, if I felt I had to be in charge and have all the answers, I would be prevented from receiving the very guidelines I needed.

With the ego firmly in control, I would continually make the mistakes that ego always causes us to make in its insistence on self-protection and fear. Letting go of fear, however, is not easy.

I was afraid that I would never get another job. That people here would never learn to trust me, and I might have to give up architecture altogether and wait tables like my kids were doing.

From the time we are infants and all through our upbringing we are conditioned to be afraid. What parent doesn't demonstrate fear of everything to their child? But if I really look back and remember, the little child I once was when I was very small, was filled with a fearless joyful anticipation of every next moment. That's what makes childhood so carefree and wonderful. I could feel that joy right then and there for everything that was happening in my life, but how was I going to support myself?

Religion too has a way of making fear the dominant force in our lives. After all, who wants to go to hell? In order to make us comply with the rules and regulations of religion, we are told that if we don't do what religion dictates, we'll be destined to go to hell and suffer for eternity when we die. If we behave ourselves, be good, and do what we are told, we can go to heaven and everything will be fine. The system makes sense, and it's pretty hard to argue with it.

Trouble is, when you've been so very good, always trying to do the right things and do what your parents have told you would make for success and happiness, and it doesn't turn out, then what? Where do you find the answers? For me, like many others, it has been a long road of searching – of reading and listening to what others have learned, taking the best bits of everything, and slowly, slowly letting go of fear.

As I scuttled around other people's camps, vacuuming and cleaning countless bathrooms, instead of designing them, I had to continually remind myself to listen — deeply – especially to my own heart. The heart is not the brain, but it is definitely a place of knowing, if we only learn to listen.

Listening deeply meant paying attention when I had a feeling deep inside my very being. This deep-heart knowing is sometimes called a "gut feeling". When I had a gut feeling, I just knew. I may not have the facts to back it up, or even any reason to believe that way, but I just knew. It's also like the "chemistry" of falling in love, you just have the feeling whether you chose to or not. It is there, and you can't deny it, or push it away. It changes you physically, you start to sweat, your heart beats faster, you get a little excited and breathless and you don't even know why, but you can't ignore it. That's the heart messaging you.

During the entire first part of my life I learned to do what I was expected no matter what my heart was telling me. What I thought might be right for me had to be wrong, because I was told it was. Over time, I learned not to listen — to stifle that which was calling me. Time after time though, I became miserable. My heart was telling me then, "this is what happens when you don't hear me." Over and over, I was finding myself in situations that did not fit, didn't work. I was unhappy but I couldn't figure out what I was doing wrong. I thought I was doing everything right.

Sometimes it takes the most tragic of life's situations to wake us up at last and force us onto another path. Only then will we listen, because we are desperate. In the many hours and literally years of my own desperation, I continued to search for answers until I finally realized I had them all along. Not that they were all apparent and so easy to see, but they were in there, in my own heart.

As I became more comfortable in my new home place, I realized with increasing awareness that I was finally making my home where my heart was. Every day I was learning how to stop the ongoing chatter and quiet myself so I could be with whatever I needed to hear. I was redesigning my life as I redesigned my home, and it was all coming together in such a perfectly unique way.

After a long day of physical labor in other people's camps, I would practically limp home, tired to the bone. As I headed toward my tiny relic of a home in the attic of the boathouse, I would see the new house coming together before me, and the serenity of the quiet lake beyond. It was a reminder of the need for balance. I knew then that because I had done the work of listening, heeding the words of the I Ching, I was creating a balanced living environment now, and it was beautiful.

Balancing the house with its site and environment was no different than allowing my life to correspond with what my spirit needed. Insisting that all the building components be authentically true to this place and real was as I wanted to be myself, as who I really am, not some false pretense that I thought I needed to be. Giving space and volume to the living room was as giving time and attention to what was necessary to make my heart feel the love, peace and serenity it longed for. And finally, to escape the obligation to do work that I knew was not appropriate for the people I worked for, or the planet, was to find a place where I could do the right work I was trained for and destined to do.

Seeing the house and silently walking alone through the unfinished rooms I was reminded that my soul itself was finding a new home. I felt the need to find the reassurance of balancing myself and remain steady on the path I knew in my heart was right for me, even in the moments when it seemed questionable.

A quiet evening swim in the lake was always a reliable means to soothe my wavering sense of peace. As I floated out into the soft clear water, I could see all the way down to the round, age-old rocks below, their shapes formed by glaciers that had once been here centuries ago. There were the remains too of ancient cribbing that would have been the foundation for a long ago dock or mooring. No other water I had ever experienced was as clean, clear and healing as was this. Turning in the water and looking back at the house emerging from the woods all around it, I could feel myself gently being brought into harmony with it all. With a deep breath, I allowed myself to relax with the intuition that everything was as it should be, and right with the world.

One day I got a call from my realtor in Virginia, and she gave me the unexpected news that a contract had been placed on my house there. She had a buyer and was faxing the agreement to a lawyer in town so that I could go into his office, review it, sign it, and return it. I was absolutely thrilled. The market had been so dead, there had been no offers at all the entire time we had had it listed. This wasn't the deal of the century, but it meant that I could actually move house, and create my new office and practice in New York.

As soon as I had called to determine that I could see the lawyer right then, I dropped everything and drove to his office. He had known me for a while because he was Tina's lawyer, but I had not needed him for any legal matters so far.

I parked the car, practically skipped into the office, and was met by his wife who is also his right hand person. She said, "Your contract is already here!" and handed it to me.

As I examined it I felt a surge of elation overcoming me. The two of them looked at me and he said, "This is one happy woman!"

It was so true and I felt my whole body exuding that happiness. I was so glad that I wasn't afraid to show it. This was the moment I had not even dared to hope for, my house was going to be sold and I was on my way to making the biggest change of my life.

We had further negotiations to make before everything was completely settled, but I knew that was routine. Inspections had to be made, fees paid, and decisions made on the little things, but just knowing that they wanted my house as much as I wanted to be in my new one was all that really mattered. I had been given the gift of release from all that was past, to all that was to come.

The summer was coming to an end, and the cool weather flowed down upon us from further north, carrying on its winds beginnings of autumn. There were bright red leaves on a few of the trees overhanging the road, and others beginning to turn yellow and bright orange. The contrast between those and the dark green of the forest shadows was stunning. Farm markets were display-ing late summer produce, and occasionally the waft of chimney smoke scented the cooling air. At night I bundled up in warm blankets, and felt the cool autumn breeze against my face as I slept above the cooling waters of the lake.

The kids and I had our last dinners together, and they said their goodbyes, anxious again to get on the move and back to all their old friends and the university they loved. While I hated to see them go, I was so proud of them for all their accomplishments, and for following their own dreams, like they were seeing me do.

Plumbing, mechanical, and wiring had been going into the house the last few weeks of summer and just before Labor Day, as crisp coolness took over the air. The insulation was complete. Knotty pine that would grace all the walls and ceilings was being finished at another location so that when it was installed it would also be finished, but I would be responsible for finishing all the doors and trim, on site. The crew set the heavy solid fir and glass doors up on sawhorses upstairs, so that we could separate the work of finishing them from saw dust that would be present as the downstairs work was being done. I hated to be separated from all the fun, but it couldn't be helped. All the doors needed three to five coats, with at least a day to dry between, and a sanding, so I had my work cut out for me. It was starting to get cold, and I had to work with my hands beginning to feel the drop in temperatures.

By the time the big doors were ready to be hung, the finishing of the trim was ready to be started. All the windows and interior doors were to have two coats with a sanding in between. I liked being amongst the crew again, but did not enjoy working from a ladder, as I had to do for all of the high windows.

When the Labor Day weekend was coming to a close, I had to bundle up a little to stay warm all night in the boathouse. I was grateful to be able to unhook the big windows facing the water and drop them down to keep the warmth in. All around the lake, camps were being closed down and made ready for the winter. Boats were taken in, shutters closed, and flags that had flown merrily all summer were lowered and brought in.

The owners of Omega came to me and told me that they wanted me to move myself back into their camp after they left to go home. They had observed the construction process all summer, and began to feel afraid to think of my staying on in the boathouse with the cold weather coming quickly upon us. I was ever so grateful! My time in the boathouse had been a wonderful experience, one I would look back upon fondly forever, but the thought of a bathroom and hot shower close at hand, not to mention a fireplace and some actual heat, was just too enticing. Once again I had been given the exact situation I needed, at the exactly right time, and I was overwhelmed with gratitude. I prepared to move again.

This time all I needed were a few personal things. I could leave the little boathouse home intact for future camp visitors. The construction of the house was in its final phases, so I planned to actually move into it over the Christmas break, when the kids would have time off from school in December. I needed them to work with me as a team, because hiring a moving company wasn't in the budget! We would have to band together and do it all ourselves, and the task was daunting.

The autumn months came, and we continued trimming and finishing the house while the leaves colored, and then fell. Cotton gave way to soft, warm flannels, thick socks and even light gloves. Once again the lake turned bitterly cold, and the adult loons left for their winter habitations. The baby loons had turned miraculously into adolescents, but they were gray and still seemed small and too young to be so alone out on the freezing waters fending for themselves. Tina and I took the last fall kayak trips to see the lowering waters, beautiful rocks thus exposed, and the fading colors. The old boulder in the cove began to rise up out of the lake again. We said our goodbyes to the young loons and prayed that they would be able to find their way to a safe waters, and find their way back to us again in spring. As October rolled in, most of the visitors were long gone until the next summer season.

When Thanksgiving came, I went to the house in Virginia to see the kids who only had a few days off from school, and began packing everything up for the sale of the house and the move. Determined to simplify our life, I spent hours sorting through everything so that I could donate things I no longer needed, throw out what was unusable, and take the bare minimum. Sometimes it was hard to let go of things I had enjoyed for so long, but if I determined they would no longer serve me in my new life, out they went, for the use of another person. The kids did the same for their things. Packed boxes lined the walls of each room. In the kitchen we made a huge stack of items to be picked up by Hospice, for donation to their thrift stores.

I really wanted to spend our first Christmas in the new lake house, so three days before Christmas, the two kids, a family friend and I took up the huge endeavor of moving out of the house in Virginia. Most of our belongings were boxed and ready to go. We thought we were prepared, but the amount of work it took was so much more than we ever anticipated, when moving day actually came.

When the last thing was packed into the rental truck and our cars, I walked slowly through all the rooms to say goodbye. This too had been a special house I had designed especially for the kids and me, so we were leaving many emotional memories behind. It had been perfect for us, and was still beautiful. I closed the door softly and turned into the light of my new beginning.

As we crossed the state line into New York the exhilarating feeling of having arrived at my home hit me. Deep snow and frigid temperatures welcomed us. When we reached the entrance into the Adirondack Park, the snowy trees and blue ice hanging off craggy rocks created a wondrous scene at every curve in the road, frozen lakes on each side. I wondered what depth the snow might be on the driveway when we got there, and remembered that none of the inexperienced truck drivers among us was willing to attempt to back the cumbersome truck down the narrow and occasionally steep driveway. But nothing could really interfere with the intense happiness of traveling with all my earthly goods and my precious kids to our new wilderness home. Everything before me brought a smile to my face. The voice of Andrea Bochelli accompanied by the horn of Chris Botti on my CD player heralded our arrival in Old Forge, just minutes away from Inlet.

My cell phone rang and an eager voice asked, "Is that you in front of me?"

In my rear view mirror was a familiar black truck with a big yellow plow attached to its front. Paul said, "Meet me with the truck in front of your place. I've got to pick up a few things."

I called the kids and told them where to pull over and wait with the truck, for help in getting it down the snowy driveway to the door. Within a few minutes we were there and I could see their visible relief when they jumped down from the cab into ankle deep snow. They ran down to the house to see it for the first time since they had left in fall for school. I knew they wouldn't be disappointed.

I felt like a three year old on Christmas morning! I found myself jumping up and down to keep warm, but really it was for pure joy.

Maneuvering the awkward truck backwards down the driveway was going to be tricky at best. When Paul pulled over he considered the challenge for a moment and said, "I think I'm gonna plow that driveway one more time before we try to take the truck down."

Before I knew it he was back from plowing. He parked his own truck and jumped up into the cab of the big moving truck while I stood guard incase we needed to stop any traffic on the main road. He cautiously but expertly backed the unwieldy vehicle right up and over the entrance hill and on down to the house in a matter of minutes. I jumped in my car and followed.

We were home!

You can create a world around you
like a temple or a house of the spirit.
Act from your heart.
— 37, I Ching

EIGHT

Although we were moving in, the lake house was far from finished. The outside was perfect in its fresh cedar shingles and gracious metal roof, an apron of snow surrounding it.

The truck was backed as close to the door as possible, so the boys laid the big metal ramp down and began to carry boxes into the house. When I walked in with the first one, the lights were on and people were working. The plumber and his helper were there adjusting the heat and install-ing the first of the bathroom fixtures. Not that they were ready to use. That would be another few more days. I inhaled the sweet smell of pine that pervaded the house, with a smile. The newly finished floors shined softly in reflected light.

We made endless trips up and down the cold metal ramp from the truck, through the winter chill and into the house, taking everything as close as we could to its designated final location. Kinan and Mayan set up my bed for me. They worked well into the evening, and after devouring some late night take- out supper, took off for the camp next door, where they had been welcomed to some beds next to a gas fireplace, with a tv, for the night. I kept moving boxes around and trying to set a few pieces of furniture in place until I too gave in to exhaustion and fell into bed. Everything was still a big confused mess.

The next day the truck was due in Utica nearby, but it wouldn't start. The rental company told us to just leave it there until they were able to come pick it up, and we wouldn't be charged for the extended time. I was amazed that it had brought us to where we needed to be, then died right there.

It was Christmas Eve, so the kids and their friend went to his home near Syracuse for his family's annual party. It was a highly anticipated gathering of friends and family, replete with lots of good food and drink, and they certainly deserved some fun. The last thing I wanted was to leave the brand new home I had just come to, so I set up my armchair, the old wooden coffee table, and lots of candles to light in celebration of the night before Christmas.

It was so much fun putting everything into place, that I couldn't stop unpacking and settling. With major furniture pieces having been set already in the room they were meant to be in, I couldn't help but try things this way and that, till I was satisfied with the placement. I loved for things to be set symmetrically in a room, but that wasn't always possible in a small house, so I had to compromise. Many of my old things from the previous house had been given away because the new rooms were smaller, and I wouldn't miss them. I had been willing to simplify my life, and that meant paring down in the home too.

Paul stopped by to check on us, and shook his head at the array of boxes everywhere. He watched me lay down the living room rug, and pull it back and forth till it seemed centered on the room and fireplace. He joked, "it looks pretty good in here except that couch is about an inch off center there…"

There was no kitchen in place, but the plumbers managed to hook up a bathroom for me. I could wash a dish or glass or two in the bathroom sink until the cabinets were ready to be delivered and the kitchen installed.

It was a wonderful feeling to be celebrating Christmas Eve at our new home! There was no tree or decorations, but when I stepped out onto the deck for a breath of bracing, cleansing air, the beautiful serenity of the woods and the frozen white lake under the moon and shimmering stars was as pretty as a Christmas card. I lit the candles and sat down to rest and write in my journal. It was my own way of winding down, re-balancing again. My entire body ached with exhaustion from the trial of moving the past two days, but I was so very happy to be at home at last.

Home.

When I looked around me there were belongings everywhere, and the unfinished pieces of the house loomed as a reminder of all the work still ahead, but I didn't care. The most beautiful thing was that I was finally where my heart had longed to be for a lifetime.

I remembered the many years I had lived the way I thought I should, trying to please others – even with colors, fabrics and furniture that suited some one else, not me. I was so focused on making them happy, even if I wasn't, that I put my own wishes aside. It didn't work. I had come to see that doing things for some one else can never make them love you. That worthiness ultimately had to come from within. Finally, it was beginning to shine through, and with it an inner joy that pervaded everything!

I would never have to use the color "gray" again. I could bring cream, butter yellow, red, and even shell pink into the house if I wanted to. My house could unapologetically reflect a soft femininity that I identified with. Light uplifting colors would be perfectly offset by the natural pine walls, pale maple floors, and the calming influence of the snowy white and deep greens of the woods beyond. I was finally free to let my environment reflect my own true spirit, in every way.

The kids returned the next afternoon for our very first Christmas together in our new place. It was exceedingly modest. We were all still very tired, but we sat together in the sun lit living room and opened the small but practical gifts we had found for each other. I got them mittens, warm socks, and knitted hats. They got me a memory card for my camera, and a DVD of my favorite old movie, Bambi. We ate Chinese take out for dinner. Unusual Christmas fare for sure, but it tasted so good to the three of us as we christened our brand new home together in the fading evening light, and toasted to our new beginning. Through the big windows we watched the light slip away between the trees, and the expanse of lake turn to blue-violet. Candle lights flickered in the glass. It was Christmas in the wilderness, but we felt snug in our brand new home.

Over the next week the kids set up their own beds and arranged their belongings in their rooms, then they headed out back down south for a few activities with their friends before the spring semester was set to begin.

I was alone again, but the crew arrived early every morning to continue with the finishing of the final details, so I had to be on my toes for them, dressed and ready for work when they got there.

Together we got the new fireplace working, and completed trimming out the house. I put together light fixtures and they hung them – each one a sparkling new delight to see. I struggled with the installation of all the bronze interior door hardware, and the electrical plates. We pulled the heavy kitchen appliances into place in the kitchen, dragging them on soft rugs to protect the new floors. My vintage oak drawing table and mission library table and desk were set up in the study, ready for work when it came in.

Every day something new was added or completed. It was all coming together. Once again it seemed that once all the major pieces of the puzzle were solved, the well-planned details fell into place naturally, without effort.

At last the recycled old hickory plank cabinets and cherry wall shelves were ready, and the craftsmen who made them set them into place with precision. The new kitchen began to materialize right before my eyes and it was even more beautiful than I had hoped! All the wood was kept its natural color to reflect the woods it had come from, a bit of roughness sanded out, and coated lightly with polyurethane to protect it. The old porcelain sink took the place of honor beneath two tall windows that brought the woods right into the space, where it could be a part of the place it seems we spend most of our time – mindfully doing dishes. My old camp dishes, bowls, baskets and tins took their places on bark trimmed cherry shelves, supported by hand fashioned bark brackets, on either side of the big sink. A collection of wooden animals, and old camp accessories assembled over many years, accompanied the everyday kitchen things. Etched glass lamps hanging from fabric cords lit up the workspace, a glowing cherry countertop. Everything was made from the most natural materials we could find, and the fixtures were chosen to be indistinguishable from the old ones still found in original Adirondack camps.

A long distressed white table I had used for years was placed right in the middle of the kitchen. Unmatched refinished chairs that had been rescued from the trash by a local craftswoman provided seating. Everyone always wants to be in the kitchen where the food is, so it's the perfect place to join with friends to prepare and cook, or get the kids and their entourage of friends and work mates to eat together to share their joys, or commiserate over sorrows. The kitchen table always brings us together. It's the same one we've eaten at since the kids were little. My old rush seated rocking chair is always pulled up to the end, so I can sit back and rock as I enjoy long after dinner conversations. A lot of things can come to light while loved ones are relaxed, eating.

The kitchen is open to the living room, and shares its light, views, and the crackle of fire in the fireplace. On its lake side is a comfortable screened porch made of big square solid fir posts, with a cedar floor. A pair of fir French doors can be opened from the kitchen out to the porch to expand the kitchen to the entire outdoors, truly opening up the family area we spend so much time in.

The porch rests beneath the canopy of a gracious pine tree whose limbs literally touch the screens and fill one's senses with the fragrance of the forest. It's the perfect summer living room, and a great spot for an afternoon nap or a good night's sleep outside. The kids insisted upon a screened porch after spending many a summer night on their friends' porches, when there were too many to accommodate inside. It was one of their favorite summer memories.

The living room opens the house completely to the lake and the forest, with long windows and transoms above, on two sides, a tall stone fireplace on the interior wall, and the kitchen adjoining it. The ceiling is vaulted, with triangular glass in the gable end, Adirondack style. The glass brings in the Great Eastern Sun as it rises over the lake every morning, and traces it all day till it sets. There is nothing more beautiful than seeing the soft glow of the sun over the mountains and lake before it rises, while the loons are waking up the world, and then the fiery ball of orange rising and reflecting over the surface of the water at daybreak. There is a sense of sacredness to the space, with its steep peaked ceiling reminding me of a little forest chapel, the scent of pine, and the outdoors coming right into the room. It gives new meaning to the word, "living room", because it is truly a room in and encompassing the living world around it.

The kids each have a modest bedroom upstairs, with a shared bath in between. Everything is pine up there too, so its simplicity needs no decoration. Just the keepsakes and treasures they both love, to bring them the sense of being in their own private space – the comfort of really being at home where they can be who they are, nurtured and loved beyond measure...

Finally, there is one more special place – and it had to be the place I would always find peace — my own room. I located it off the living room on the first floor, right beside the woods, with a view through to the lake. Windows on the southeast side match those of the living room, and create a wall of glass so I could feel the warmth and light of the sun as it rises to greet me every morning. There's barely room for anything but the bed, a rocker and a small dresser, but heirloom quilts and artwork given to me years ago make it a sanctuary from the world.

Birds flutter all over the feeders hanging from the eaves in winter, waking me and Iona early every morning. When the feeders have to come down because bears might come to investigate, their presence is replaced by the stunning calls of the wild through the open windows all summer. The owls question, "who cooks for youuuu?" and the loons make all variety of conversation, every night.

My favorite time of day is the early morning, when I take my time rising so I can watch the wildlife in all its glory. Meditating with them is heavenly, for they call upon my own inner silence with the sense of reverence I have for them. I can see the dawn come up with its soft glow over the lake, and then the bright ball of illumination of the sun itself as it makes its appearance reflecting in the water and gliding slowly across the eastern sky through the trees beside my bed. It's the perfect time for meditation, then a cup of hot tea and a few moments with a spiritually inspiring book or some poetry. To give myself this special time is to learn to love myself, to be gentle and kind with my own precious heart and soul. The day may be full of things planned, and what I may need to do for others, but the morning belongs to me.

My own room is receptacle for new energy coming into the house. Crystals line the windowsills, like on an altar, receiving the blessings of the sun. As they are energized, they in turn cleanse and positively energize the space. The windows are free of curtains or shades, but instead are hung with the gourd, stone, bead, bell and crystal hangings of a local Native American woman. A medicine wheel made by Native Americans in North Carolina hangs right over my head when I sleep, to heal my body and soul. An inked calligraphy of the mantra, "Truth" hangs above the headboard, draped with a protection cord given to me by the Sakyong Mipham, at KarmeCholing.

Returning to my room is like coming home, over and over. It refreshes and provides me the comfort, peace and serenity I need every day.

On the outside of the house, natural red cedar shingles, aging to their soft patina, allow the house to blend with the woods. There are generous over-hangs to protect the interior from overheating in the summertime, and to project the snow out in the winter. All the trim is natural pine and every-thing is lightly coated with a transparent stain solution so that natural aging of the wood pro-vides the color. An extra deep bronze metal roof rises in a steep pitch that adds to the grace of the building. Fir and cedar porches provide shelter at the doorways and store the endless stacks of fire-wood needed to warm the house in winter. From the lake, the house appears tucked gently into the woods, and seems to be emerging from it.

I have always felt that upon visiting a house, it would "speak to me", letting me know what it wanted. I, in turn, wanted to provide that for the house and for the family that would live in it, giv-ing it life. After so many years of doing that, I had wanted this new house to "speak of me." — to be the embodiment of my heart. As I settled in, I could feel that my heart was right at home.

The winter months passed into spring, the sense of new beginnings and the feeling that every detail was right, pervaded everything. I was not only in the house of belonging, but the place too.

Mindfulness is a kind of energy you can produce, it's the energy that brings your mind back to your body, so you can live your life more deeply.
— Thich Nhat Hanh

NINE

As the house became complete and work began to wind down, the crew finished everything they needed to do, and didn't come to the house to work anymore. Paul went on to his other projects. They left me to myself in the brand new house, to settle in and make it my very own home.

It was like heaven being in the new place, but I missed the camaraderie, and the company of the team of friends that had become almost like family to me. All of a sudden, everything went quiet. The peaceful silence was beautiful, but new challenges began to emerge.

Not many people live in the Adirondack Park year around. In the spring, fondly called "mud season", the snow begins to melt, so snowmobiling and skiing come to an end. The few people who do live here and have work that serves the visiting vacationers get a break between the long winter's hospitality trade, and the coming summer season. Restaurants and businesses close, and people try to get away for a personal break. That can leave the place feeling a bit empty and bare. As Tina would say, "You can lie down and take a nap on route 28 (the main street through town) and no one would run over you".

The sudden sense of aloneness I felt after nine months of busy, productive, active days was surprising, and profound. It was more than being alone – it was very close to isolation. With no neighbors on either side of the camp, all the storefronts quiet and empty, and seemingly not a soul in sight, the sense of aloneness became something of a presence, a force to be reckoned with. Meetings and gatherings were suspended, and it began to feel like a long time since the kid's voices chimed in the house. But summer break was still a way off. I had to develop a fierce sense of self-reliance to get through the many days of being pretty much alone all day and night, till the season would change again. It may have been good to take a short trip away for the relief of seeing old friends, family, and a change of scene, but that wasn't possible because of architectural work that was just beginning to come in.

Solitude becomes a presence.

Yes, I was home, but could I learn to be with just myself?

I began to search for ways to find the inner strength to be just me, alone in the moment.

In the early mornings I looked out at the woods and the winter birds feverishly swarming the feeders, and they seemed my only companions. I had to feel the solitude of the wilderness, with all of its silent beauty and wonder, and remember why I had come there. Every day I saw the wide white expanse of snow covered ice on the lake, searching for emerging ponds of water on the surface left by a brief rain, or the breakthrough melting of a warm sunny morning. It seemed forever that the frozen lake would stubbornly cling to the rocky shores and refuse to let go. I wanted to will the clear spring ice water to appear at the shore, signaling the beginning of the ice going out. It almost seemed that I had forgotten what the blue shining summer lake looked like.

I sought comfort by going deeply within myself, for silent meditation and prayer. I prayed for strength for myself, and for peace within my aching heart. With gratitude for all that I had been given, I asked for the serenity I needed to truly let go of the past with all its conditional behavior patterns, and embrace the life I'd been given in this glorious place, in the moment. I prayed for the safety, good health, and peace I longed for for my children, knowing that I couldn't give that to them.

I remembered that Chogyam Trungpa Rinpoche taught his students that extreme loneliness is necessary to awakening, which cannot be achieved with a companion. He taught that you have to be truly alone because being half lonely means you are constantly trying to fill the empty half with something. He said that aloneness is the heart of discipline. You see your own helplessness and you have to make friends with it. You have no choice. You don't choose aloneness, it comes to you and becomes your helpful path. You discover an inspiration and devotion that is rich and resourceful.

As I meditated, and prayed throughout the day, peace began to come to me. My inner voice emerged and spoke to me. I began to relax with the silence, and embrace it. I remembered how important it was to attain balance, not going to the extremes of depression or great happiness, but just being strong in the center. Just being.

I practiced self-reiki every day, to soothe my body and my tender heart. I stretched with yoga poses, took long walks in the woods, and held my face up to the sun whenever it graced my presence, letting it warm me and melt everything into springtime.

These changes didn't come easily. I had to struggle with emotions that were emerging. I did not have the routine distractions that used to keep me busy so I did not have to think. I was in the place I wanted to be, so why was an overlay of sadness threatening to rest on my shoulders? Sometimes I fought the tears as I looked out the window through the woods and watched the birds skip and play together. My children were a long distance from me now and I couldn't just hop in the car to go see them, or expect them to come to me for any weekend visits. I had to stick it out, and work with it. I had to learn self- acceptance, and to really be in the moment.

I remembered the practice of being with pain, the unpleasantness, rather than trying to drive it away. I acknowledged and looked at my feelings with a gentle understanding, saying to myself, "Aloneness. This is aloneness, and though it may make me sad, it will pass. I will let it go." I accepted the way I felt, because it was where I was right then, and it was okay. The more I embraced my actual feelings rather than judge them to be somehow wrong or shameful, the less power they had over me. I began to find peace in that acceptance, and then later even joy in each new day, no matter what it would bring. The experience helped me to practice and become more skilled at being in the moment with mindful awareness.

And so that part of me that had once, long ago been trained to reject what I was feeling, came forth to help, support, and heal me.

As the slowly emerging spring made its appearance – like the details in an old Hokusai print, a tiny bud here, a delicate rivulet there — I began to take tremendous joy in everything that signaled a new time. The ice began to slip from the shore-line, allowing a bigger and bigger circle of freezing blue water to surround the shore. Dark earth began to show at the base of trees, which marked the time that the forest animals would come out from their secret places of hibernation to eat and see the new world again. The streams roared ever louder with melting waters, and it was music to my ears!

Then there's the matter of firewood.

The first winter in the new house, I was completely unprepared to use wood heat, because I had not planned on it and had never ordered firewood at all. It was not until spring that all the wiring in the ceiling of the basement was completed so that the floor insulation could be installed to keep the radiant heating tubes reflecting all of their precious heat in the cavity of the first floor. So, when the bills for propane came in each month I was stunned at the cost of relying totally on propane heat as fuel for the system, though I loved comfort of the radiant floors.

Spring was imminent, but spring in the mountains is still a lot like winter for what seems to be an awfully long time.

Each time I was able to get the wood stove stoked properly though, the radiant heat would subside as the fan of the wood stove blew warm air into the spaces sufficient to carry the entire burden of heating the house. The stove is a hybrid type of wood stove that is framed in, finished as desired – mine with stone, and a wild wood mantel that Paul made, so that it looks just like a masonry fireplace with cast iron and glass doors. A thermostat starts the fan when heat in the stove is hot enough, and turns it off when the fire is cooling or going out. It is amazingly efficient as a whole house heating system.

Trouble is, I had to work with firewood day and night, and that seemed to absorb so much time, energy and focus. In time I found I needed ten face chords of wood to heat the house for the season. In the fall, this wood was dumped in a huge pile in my driveway, and it only made sense for me to stack it myself. Three quarters of it fit on my back porch under roof, where it is convenient to the door. There's a stacking ring just inside the door. The rest had to go elsewhere in the yard nearby, covered until there was room for it on the porch later. All this had to be done in time for the wood to have a chance to season before it was needed.

Off course wood had to be moved inside from the porch about every four days. Then, it had to be carried to the hearth, ready to use – two more trips.

If I relied totally on wood heat, it required getting up at night to feed the stove. It was like having a newborn in the house – I never got a full night of sleep, having to get up several times, depending on bedtime. I was very frustrated for lack of a good sleep. The winter dragged on like it would never end, and I was very tired.

It was yet another lesson in acceptance, to work with wood every day with the Zen phrase "chop wood, carry water," ringing constantly in my head. The very act of doing everyday tasks could be a source of meditative contemplation. I decided to use this chore, just like doing the dishes, as a way to deepen my path. By changing my perception, I was able to stack and carry wood as an important part of my every day.

First thing in the morning I laid a new fire while tea brewed in the china pot. It became a routine task that I could shift my focus to, rather than allowing my mind to gravitate toward with resentment. As the fire began to crackle, I would sip the hot tea and sit with the comfort and understanding that I was taking responsibility for the heating energy in my own home, myself. I had resisted the urge to simply switch on the propane, sitting back and waiting to be warmed – instead I was taking part in the concept of energy conservation I had stood for all of my life. The powerful heat from the stove felt so good and warmed me — body and soul.

Another very interesting aspect of my new life in the Adirondacks was living with wild animals. Unlike in more "civilized" places, the animals of the wilderness are part of everyday experience. Does and fawns stroll the edges of the roadways and indeed meander into the streets of the villages. One has to use caution for them, just as for human pedestrians. There are wild turkeys, ospreys, herons, eagles, and myriad birds that visit frequently, and of course the loon families that are so beloved. Bobcats, coyotes, foxes, moose, otters, and mink, are all part of the forests and lakes, and then there is the king of earth, the bear.

The first time I saw a bear, she was sitting down in the middle of the driveway eating from the little wildflowers that grew there. She got up and meandered through the woods to see what the neighbor's yard had to offer, and then passed back to return in the direction she had come, this time sniffing her way along the lake's edge. I was amazed at her silky black beauty, her calm demeanor.

Later, two bears came together exploring the shoreline of the lake through all the camps that edged it. One looked really big and older with a slightly graying face, and the other a bit smaller and younger. These two passed through, foraging quietly and seeming to know just where they were headed, numerous times. I was so careful to never have any trash outdoors, and to even keep the smells of anything that might attract them as enclosed into the camp as I could. Because of the way that we humans had allowed and even encouraged bears to feed on trash in the past, they are always in search of an easy snack from trash, and can cause a great deal of destruction getting to something that attracts them. Now there are laws discourage prevent humans from feeding bears and deer, but sometimes people still do it.

It is an honor to share the wilderness with the wild animals for whom this unique habitat is home. I have learned to respect their presence utterly. They were here first, and belong here. We are the visitors. While I was afraid at first that a bear might want to come into the house and harm me, by appreciatively observing them I learned that they are really not interested in humans, and only want to go about living with as little contact with us as possible.

Animals leave areas of construction during the time when the noise and presence of people scares them away. But in time, when the activity disappears and a dwelling begins to fit into the environment, they re-appear. They come cautiously at first, even the birds. It takes a long time before the wild creatures feel safe enough to wander out of the secure protection of the woodlands close enough for people to enjoy them. But once they do, they become an integral part of what makes for a joyfully unique existence in the wilderness.

Across my property the animals have made clear trails that they use regularly to pass through the camps along the lake. They are part of who lives here, and never cease to amaze me in their gentle magnificence.

As I have become more and more accustomed to the wilderness, I have found a deep reverential respect for nature here in all of it's wonder. God is in the details of every feathery wing or branch, every claw, hoof and paw, and in the interaction all these living things have upon each other and the humans who come to share their sacred home. It is our duty and responsibility to protect this unique setting and all of its creatures, for they came before us and should rightfully endure when we are gone.

*A new moon teaches gradualness and deliberation
and how one gives birth to oneself slowly.
Patience with small details makes perfect
a large work, like the universe.*

— Rumi

TEN

pring brought tiny wildflowers that began to pop up in the forest, and I simply couldn't resist the lure of long walks. Every chance we got, Tina and I played hooky from life's chores and took the dogs over the wet and somewhat muddy old trails, just to be able to feel the light warm breeze on our faces and see everything changing. The streams and creeks were once again rushing with icy water stumbling over rocks and splashing everywhere. Mats of delicate green moss were revealed by the melting snow, and old copper pine needles softened our steps underfoot. Brand new buds were bursting in the woods and Tina would take great joy in being able to name just about all of them. She's a life long naturalist, and can be depended upon to have a book of matches and a little knife in her pocket wherever she goes. Just in case. As a newcomer to the wilderness, I had a lot to learn, and she showed me by example how to be safe and well prepared when out on a hike or in a boat.

The ice "went out" of the lakes in mid April. It was hard to keep from dashing into the frigid water with your canoe or kayak when that happens, but I had learned to apply patience and wait for the sun and the water to warm up a little. There is nothing worse than to be caught off guard in the middle of a long paddle when a stiff storm comes up, and it suddenly feels a lot more like winter than springtime! You just can't get warm, and you find yourself struggling to get back safely to shore as fast as possible, when a little fear and panic sets in. You only have to experience that a few times to begin to remember you don't want to have that feeling again, especially when alone.

So, Tina and I began longingly planning our boat trips in advance of good weather, like a gardener looking through the seed catalogs in the middle of winter. There are so many gorgeous lakes and streams to explore, and of course the black and white loons with their bright red eyes to watch as they make their return to the usual spots and select a nesting place.

That first spring we found a pair down the far end of Seventh Lake who made their nest in a bog down a fairly quiet channel. We saw the egg and the birds taking turns sitting. We knew that the egg would hatch in good time.

One day when we paddled down there to see how they were doing, the tiny chick was resting on his mother's back as she floated proudly around the nesting area. The father was in the near distance, fishing and keeping his eye on things. The baby was remarkably small but was already sliding off his mother's back and swimming close beside her. We could see the off-white eggshells still in the nest, so we knew his birth must have been very recent.

I am always amazed at the relationship a loon pair has. They feed each other and their baby, and take turns nesting and caring for their young. It is a beautiful thing to see one of the parents dive under water, come up with a delicate little fish and put it into the mouth of the baby. Then take a turn watching baby as the other loon goes fishing for something to eat, and a break from "childcare". They are devoted to the care of each other, and amazingly, are better mates and parents than some people I know.

It would be such a privilege to observe the growing baby loon all summer, and as I floated there gently in my kayak I could imagine the cycle of the season ahead. Very quickly after his birth this chick would be diving underwater for his own fish, just like his parents. He would stay very close to them, but sometimes a parent would call quietly to him so he would know immediately where to come when he popped up from a dive. Watching the loons is a favorite pastime in the Adirondack waters. In their own unique language, I would hear them calling back and forth all summer, and I would picture them perfectly as they swam together all over the lake, day and night.

Paddling back to camp, something deep inside was sounding like a clear-voiced bell. The sky overhead was shining blue, full of spring breeze, birdsong, the first scent of something blooming was off in a mysterious wooded glade, and the air fairly crackled with a delicate energy.

It was life itself, breaking all around me... through me. My whole body tingled.

As I neared the shore coming home I saw something truly amazing. An elegant blue heron was standing as still as a statue, on my big boulder! He was looking toward camp, as if silently guarding the cove and the camp. I could hardly believe he was real, as still as he was. According to Iroquois legend, the appearance of the great blue heron is held to be an omen of great good fortune – a lucky sign. He is a symbol of "going with the flow", working with the elements. At that moment I could do nothing but stare at this miracle, a smile of happiness all over my face.

The blessing of living in this wonderland touched my heart every morning when I woke up in its midst. I was constantly amazed that I was really there. At night I looked for the first bright star, so that I could make a wish to remember my deep gratitude for being allowed to have received the gift of this place.

Enlightenment is not a sudden thing, but
a path brought about by willingness
to respond mindfully in every moment to what
comes, and to be in alignment with it.

ELEVEN

*I*n my new life deep in the wilderness, I was reminded each day of the Three Jewels, or Three Treasures, in the Buddhist tradition, and learned to honor them in every part of my life. These are: the Buddha, finding one's own highest spiritual potential; the dharma, the blessed path or Way; and the sangha, or community of like minded people who love and support each other as we travel the spiritual path together.

Chogyam Trungpa taught that taking refuge in the Three Jewels is like waking up, but better, because it is realizing that you are already awake. There is a magical power of wakefulness that can be reflected into us.

I have felt so blessed to be in this glorious place that cannot but foster my own spontaneous buddha nature. As I learned to listen with increased care to the messages of my heart, I found that I was finally beginning to embrace the innate basic goodness in myself. It dawned on me that I didn't have to "be good", or follow the rules of cultural conditioning that I thought would make me a good person, because I was born good. All I had to do was realize that goodness is my own natural way of being, and find a way to really be with that goodness, accept it and trust in it. I was still having trouble with that, because somewhere deep in my heart, I didn't believe it.

The dharma is the path of truth. By engaging with the dharma we decide to relate to truth, committing to the natural flow of life as it is, and thus we enter the realm of spiritual power, or mystical energy. We create magic, or higher truth, with the simple practice of meditation, and tuning into it. Then magical things begin to happen, regularly.

By committing to the dharma, or spiritual path of truth, we become free, because we recognize our own sanity. We no longer follow along with the discursive thoughts and ideas the ego comes up with, supposedly to protect us.

I almost didn't find this path. Had I continued to give in to the need to lose myself in the care of others, to seek my worthiness there, I believe I would still be doing that, to no avail — endlessly searching for self worth by giving to others, almost as if attempting to buy their love, through doing things for them. Loving and giving to them everything I could, so that eventually they would just have to see how good and worthy I was, even if I didn't even actually believe it myself. This is not authentic love of self or others. I had become so entrenched in making the right and loving plans that I was unable to listen to the intuitive messages of my heart and to let happen what needed to happen.

Now I have learned that as I travel the dharma path in my life, it is not necessary to make plans for whatever will happen next. We have to make plans, of course, but we can also make an opening as wide as the wilderness for what life wants to give. Going with the flow, or being with the moment, is an act of bravery. It is having the courage to be open to whatever comes, relaxing into the wonderful mystery. This all encompassing acceptance of my own goodness was becoming a kind of confidence and strength for me. I no longer had to doubt everything I felt, or wanted to do. I just needed to be consistent in listening deeply to see if the insight was coming from the heart, and then be open to what would happen next. While insight is spontaneous, the path of enlightenment is long term. It is a journey I was constantly working with – continually trying to recognize who I was, right now, in each moment.

Trusting and surrendering to the cosmic process is letting go of outcome. It is waking up in the morning to the gift of a brand new day, without really knowing exactly what will unfold. It is a deep inner knowing that we are all filled with basic goodness, and that there is a wonderful plan that we were made for even before being born. It is an attitude that allows us to take in everything, the bright sunny times as well as the rainy days.

Everything is not always sweetness and light. When troubles come, and they always do from time to time, it is best to remember to look at the emotions they summon, feel that pain if need be, and then let go. If fear, sadness and even tears engulf us, to be with those emotions too, recognizing them as part of us in the same way that joy is. We don't have to make the emotions go away. By relaxing with them, they diminish and eventually dissolve. Recognizing that they are transitory demonstrates the power of the mind as it matures, tames, and expands. Worry, nervousness, excitement and agitation no longer have to consume mental space. We can explore these emotions when they appear, knowing that they do not define us. Embracing what is there in the moment brings connection with the spirit. Balance is attained by not going too far with every little thing. It is staying in the center.

Listening mindfully to my heart has been a process that has allowed me to be present, not only in the moment, but for my own life. Nothing can be more delightful than knowing that I am just where I need to be at all times, and trusting in that. It is like being led by the hand of the universe to where I need to go, without knowing exactly where that will take me. It is believing and trusting in the plan that I have been made for. Not having to know all the answers is so freeing, and that to me is where true happiness begins to arise.

When things are easy, I know I am on the path. If big obstacles come up, things get difficult, or I am ill, I know that I need to re-balance myself. It is like walking on a beam of light – my true self just knows how to regain balance again whenever I waver. It comes naturally by listening deeply all the time so that I can receive the guidance that is right there on the spot.

With everything I encounter, whether it is a lull in work and income, a proliferation of work that I can hardly get finished, a kindly new person I meet, or an old friend who has problems, the response is always the same. Look deeply, listen, and be with what is being presented in the moment, for it is always part of the master plan even if I can't see it right then. There is no need to jump on the roller coaster of "this is wonderful" or "this is unbearable", for whatever "this" is, will pass. To rely on inner strength, along with the discipline of meditation, is to stay in the center. All the answers will come in due time. Balance is in the yin and yang of life, the increase and the decrease, the joy and yes – the sorrow too. It is all a part of life's mysterious illusion.

Becoming awake initiates a desire to share this precious knowledge with others, to make the offering of enlightenment to loved ones and friends, to plant and nurture its seeds. How does one do this?

For this I needed the third Jewel, the sangha of a supportive, nurturing, strengthening community, where we can start. Like-minded friends can become beacons for each other, like rays of the sun. The sangha can be a place of retreat where one can feel comfortable and safe speaking the truth – a place of non judgmental acceptance.

I have been so blessed to have found a group of friends right here in my new home who embody the spirit of love, and are willing to share it regularly, devotedly. The group meets once a week during the lunch hour so that even those working full time can spare an hour to find solace and comfort, or extend support to those in need at any given time. We inspire each other to be happy and are willing to step back to take the hand of anyone of us who may need a little encouragement when difficulties arise. There is never a time when I haven't felt increased confidence, determination, and love when I have departed our group meetings.

When there was a death in my family I sought the companionship of this wonderful group of women who could share my grief with me. We all met, coming together by car and by boat, on one friend's dock in the late summer's sun one afternoon. By sharing our true emotions, we found the common ground we all have together when sorrow embraces us. I had lost my nephew, and suffered the loss with my sister and her husband, but at the same time others of our group were suffering a similar grief over their troubled children, or difficulties we all face in families. My loved ones reminded me of the reason to let sadness go, with the knowledge and faith in a perfect cosmic plan that was unfolding before me.

With the loving support of sangha, I can be alone, knowing that I am never alone. I can share what I have learned, in the spirit of true love, and receive the love our universe offers.

The long winters have taught me the real meaning of being alone. The teachings of Trungpa Rinpoche encouraged me to go further into my spiritual practice. I knew that even though I was in the exact place I needed to be, that there was more I needed to know. I went to my own library and selected each of his books, one by one, and re-read them. There was new meaning for me in all of his teachings. I read that being in pain suggested the need to go deeper with that pain. Rather than trying to avoid it, trying to find a way out of it — to take it on, and find the true miracle that lay within it.

In the deep solitude of the cold long winters, it seemed that I was experiencing all the pain I could take, but I had not found the understanding I really needed. I knew there was something more. I had the distinct feeling that there was another important step I needed to take, but I didn't know what that step could be.

One clear winter day while reading Shambala Sun, I learned of a retreat to be led by Chogyam Trungpa's son, the Sakyong Mipham, called Being Brave: A Shambala Retreat, to be held at Karme-Choling in Barnet, Vermont, in May. I immediately registered for it, not really knowing where the money would come from to pay the tuition to attend. I loved the Sakyong's books, Ruling Your World, and Turning the Mind Into an Ally, and had been profoundly influenced by his writing, sharing these books with my children and spiritual friends. I knew I had to go to hear what he would be teaching. It would be my next step, though I had no idea where it would take me.

I was accepted as a participant and assigned to my requested sleeping venue, the floor of the shrine room, which cost $10 a night. I thought I would be one of only a few to ask for such humble accommodations, but it turned out I was to share the space with about 80 people!

When I arrived at the peaceful meditation center that was founded by Chogyam Trungpa many years ago, I didn't know a single person, and had no idea what our program would be like for the next five days. I just knew I was supposed to be there.

I took my bag to the tiny cubicle I was to share with others in the crowded woman's changing room, and then went to look around. I had to see all the artwork and calligraphy done by Trungpa Rinproche, that was hanging on so many of the walls, so I quietly wandered around, imagining what it might have been like for him when he was there in those very rooms so long ago. To be able to see some of the work of the man I admired so much was a joyful privilege.

That evening we participants all met in the dining tent for a one-bowl dinner, and then gathered in the meditation hall to practice together for the first time, and then hear about what was planned for us for the week.

The retreat was centered around meditation, from sun-up till sun-down each day, including a talk to be given to us daily some time during the morning hours by the Sakyong Rinpoche. Although this was the brightest part of each day, and what we all looked forward to the most, we also learned every day too from conversations led by the acharyas (experienced teachers). We ate all our one-bowl meals together, either in the dining tent or the meditation hall in silence. There was to be an unexpected twenty four hour period of silence midweek, a certain challenge for us all.

When I went to the big hall that night, taking a thin mat we were given to place on the floor, I found a peaceful silence. If there was talk, it was in whispers, with total respect for all the people trying to find quiet and rest. I shined my flash-light on my book to read, but in a few moments I found I had to slip into sleep, like everyone else, snoring withstanding.

When the Sakyong appeared before us to begin his teaching the first morning, he told us, "Everything you have been doing for the last twenty years has been a waste of time". We all had a great laugh over that idea, but when I thought later about what he had said, I realized he was exactly right. He has a marvelous sense of humor… and he was about to teach us something new that we had never experienced before. It would change my life.

The Sakyong told us he would teach us a new meditation practice, with three parts: feeling, being, and touching. Here is what I learned.

About **feeling.**

The Sakyong told us that when we initiate practice, to take an inventory of how we are feeling, emotionally and physically, looking at our bodily state to note whether we are feeling great, or in pain. Do we feel comfortable, or is that hip or leg aching like it usually does? Are we ready for meditation, or tired and sleepy? Are thoughts, worries and anxieties interrupting our peaceful sitting? Perhaps we are in the habit of pushing these feelings away, so we can go on to practice.

He told us that whatever we are feeling, to look at that and accept it – not to try to get rid of the feelings and change them. To just let them be right there where they are on the spot. In fact, we can actually explore the range of these feelings, and look at each one of them.

About **being.**

The second step he taught us in initiating meditation is being. In this step we were instructed to place our hand over our heart, and just be with what is our true center, the heart. Not like a pledge of allegiance gesture, but more to the center of the chest where the fourth chakra resides, that of the heart.

For me this was a most precious gesture toward myself, a touching of the heart, the source of my existence. It is the tender, aching, wounded heart that was so overlooked and in need of loving attention. When I made the gesture for the first time, a sensation of warmth and healing instantly appeared beneath my hand, and spread all over my chest. It was calming, relaxing and soothing. There was a deep connection that let my own heart know that I myself am basic goodness, worthiness, and love. It is not something that I ever had to earn or achieve, it just is. When we are not being genuine to ourselves, we are suffering. I had experienced that suffering all of my life, going by my conditioned behavior and experience, rather than my own truth, and I didn't want to do that anymore.

About **touching**.

The third step he taught is to literally touch the earth, ground, or mat beneath you, as

Buddha did when he touched the earth beneath him at the base of the tree where he awakened. This little act of grace grounds us, lets us know we are right there where we are in that very moment. We touch the earth, and we also dip the hand into the stream of life. We are ready to go with the flow.

We touch our presence on earth here and now. We acknowledge our self, living and being here with all our flaws and more importantly, all our basic goodness, right here at this very moment.

The Sakyong repeatedly guided us through meditation with these three new pieces of practice in place, each day. For me, meditation took on a completely new meaning. I was filled with a new sense of knowing, and joy.

Over the week I felt I was finally coming to the real end of trying to change myself. In all the many years of practice I was always thinking of how I needed to be better than I am, and working toward that. I was never sure of how I was doing, getting better, or not? Was I achieving enlightenment on the step by step program? Certainly it was not going to happen for me like a bolt of lightening, like some people have said happened to them. For me, it was the process of becoming completely good, like Jesus was. That was what I thought I needed to do — become goodness.

The Sakyong gave us a way to connect with our hearts. He saw what was missing in our meditation practice, maybe for years on end, where we never knew where we were going with it, or getting with it. His inspirational message was just to go directly to the heart. The heart is the place that is our own, a place that no one else can claim. He told us, "This is mine," placing his hand over his heart. We knew that he had given so much, every part of him, to practice, since he was a little child, and to teaching. But there was a part he could reserve for himself, just as we can.

The Sakyong met with us in small groups on our last retreat day. With incense pervading our senses, we filed into the sun filled, polished shrine room and took our seats on silky red cushions as he chanted in Tibetan on a raised platform before us, as if to honor each of us. When silence came, we practiced our new initiation to meditation with him, meditating together.

Then he spoke to us as if he were talking to each of us individually. He looked deeply into our eyes as he talked softly to us, and we all listened intently. I felt his message was just for me, exactly what he wanted to tell me, and exactly what I needed to hear at that perfect moment in time.

He told us that he knew of our aspirations, our dreams. He wanted us to know that we could and would accomplish the aspirations that we held in our hearts. At that moment I was full of emotion, and amazement that he would know the pain that had continually lay hidden in my heart. He was telling me that I needed no healing at all, because my heart was already love, and basic goodness. I didn't have to find it, learn it, or work to accomplish it, for it was already there. All I had to do was know, and be with it.

As I sat in the presence of this unique experience, emotions flooded my body and soul. When it was time to leave the room, I walked out with the others shakily, but went directly outside to the pond, where I noticed that a few other individuals had come to be alone instead of returning to the group for additional meditation. I took off my sandals and walked very slowly on the cool, wet, green grass and found a spot where I could sit alone, and let my tears go. I had received the message I had longed for, for a lifetime. The knowledge that was always indeed mine, but I had been afraid to really see, "You are worthy."

What do we do with this knowledge? How can we bring it to our crazy troubled, sometimes sick and violent world? Is an enlightened society even possible, with all there is to face?

The Sakyong taught me how to make the first step, with myself. To acknowledge that I am already good, and listen to my own heart with all its goodness too. Then, I can take that message to my loved ones, my family, and the sangha.

This is the practice we can all choose to bring enlightenment, happiness and peace, to ourselves and to the world. It begins right where we are. As Sakyong Mipham asks, "Can you take the first step? Can you touch the beginning?" The answers do not have to be there for us. Just to be able to take this first step is to reach forward to embrace the beginning of change, and all that it promises.

Enlightenment begins at home, in our own hearts. We can only extend it to others by living it ourselves first. We can then share it with our loved ones, our sangha, and then finally the extended family of our world.

Peace and love for our world is entirely possible, but first we must take the first step ourselves, by listening with mindful awareness to our own heart, acknowledging the goodness we were born with, and blowing a gentle breath to nurture our eternal spark.

Made in the USA
Charleston, SC
24 June 2014